CHALLENGES OF VIOLENCE WORLDWIDE

WORLDWIDE

AN EDUCATIONAL RESOURCE

CHALLENGES OF VIOLENCE WORLDWIDE

AN EDUCATIONAL RESOURCE

Written and Compiled by
Jane Crosby and Dorothy Van Soest
For the Violence & Development Project

NASW PRESS

National Association of Social Workers
Washington, DC

Jay J. Cayner, ACSW, LSW, *President*
Josephine Nieves, MSW, PhD, *Executive Director*

_____ ices Director_

Wendy Almelen, Copy Editor
Louise Goines, *Proofreader*
Patricia D. Wolf, Wolf Publications, Inc., *Proofreader*
Angland Creek Indexing, *Indexer*

The six parts in this educational resource were developed with the assistance of six NASW chapter-based Violence and Development Project Centers and a Curriculum Development Working Group of the Council on Social Work Education's International Commission.

This publication was made possible through support provided by a Development Education matching grant, number FAO-0230-A-00-3041-00, from the Office of Private and Voluntary Cooperation, Bureau for Food and Humanitarian Assistance, U.S. Agency for International Development. The views expressed herein do not necessarily reflect those of USAID.

Library of Congress Cataloging-in-Publication Data
   Crosby, Jane.
      Challenges of violence worldwide : an educational resource /
   written and compiled by Jane Crosby and Dorothy Van Soest.
         p.   cm.
      "For the Violence & Development Project."
      Includes bibliographical references and index.
      ISBN 0-87101-269-3 (alk. paper)
      1. Violence.   2. Social problems.   3. Social policy.   4. Social
   service.   I. Van Soest, Dorothy.   II. Title.
   HM281.C88   1996   96-29541
   303.6–dc21   CIP

Printed in the United States of America

*Dedicated to Eileen McGowan Kelly
for her consistent and visionary leadership
in advancing the international dimensions of social work*

CONTENTS

PREFACE

In 1980, President Carter's Commission on Hunger found that the American public knew very little about the extent of hunger and poverty in the rest of the world. This ignorance exists despite the fact that the problem is so pervasive. Although things have steadily improved in many regions, 1.1 billion of the world's people still live in poverty. Eight hundred million are chronically hungry.

As a result of the findings of the commission, the U.S. Congress passed a law that sets aside money for programs to educate Americans about the challenges facing underdeveloped countries and efforts being made to improve living standards there.

The National Association of Social Workers (NASW), through its Peace and International Affairs program, received some of this funding in 1988 when it was awarded its first development education grant from the United States Agency for International Development (USAID). Building on five years of experience, NASW received its third USAID grant in 1993. The initiative that was subsequently launched is called the Violence and Development Project. The *Educational Resource* and *Curriculum Module* that you hold in your hands are one result of this initiative.

The main objective of the project has been to expand the context within which social workers address social problems to include a global understanding of the relationship between violence and development. Six NASW chapter-based project centers, involving 11 states, were established as part of the project. The centers engaged the talents of hundreds of their chapter members at the grassroots level in developing educational materials, educating their constituents locally and regionally on violence and development issues, and organizing teach-in activities. The project centers were the Northwest Center on Violence, Development, and Ethnicity (involving the Oregon, Idaho, and Washington NASW chapters); the New York City NASW chapter Center on Violence, Development, and Poverty; the California NASW chapter Center on Violence,

Development, and Trauma; the Florida NASW chapter Center on Violence, Development, and Trauma; the Minnesota NASW chapter Center on Violence, Development, and Women and Children; and the Midwest Center on Violence, Development, and Substance Abuse (involving the Michigan, Ohio, Illinois, and Indiana NASW chapters).

A highlight of the project came in February 1996, when a national Teach-In titled *Social Workers and the Challenge of Violence Worldwide* was held on the campuses of several hundred schools of social work in 41 states, Puerto Rico, and the Virgin Islands. Local organizers put together programs about violence and development. Two landmark national satellite video conferences were broadcast live during the week. Both programs were moderated by renowned CBS broadcast journalist Charles Kuralt. Twenty thousand social workers watched. During the second broadcast, viewers around the country interacted live via telephone with Mr. Kuralt and a panel of speakers.

From the experience of the Teach-In week, we learned that social workers are eager to study community building and global learning as a response to violence. Ninety percent of those who responded to a national evaluation felt that these topics should be incorporated into social work training at every level.

The *Educational Resource* and *Curriculum Module* are one response to this need for training. For topics as enormous as development, violence, and global interdependence, no one book contains all the answers. But these materials do represent one more step forward in the efforts of social workers to better understand and respond to a rapidly changing world. It is our hope that they will help social workers see their profession in an international context and understand that countries in the developing world, while struggling with issues and problems similar to our own, have created models and approaches that can be useful to us.

Jane Crosby and Dorothy Van Soest
August 1996

ACKNOWLEDGMENTS

The Violence and Development Project, out of which this resource evolved, is a truly collaborative one, and literally hundreds of people have been involved in shaping it.

Volunteers were the mainstay of the project. The International Activities and the Peace and Justice Committees of the National Association of Social Workers have long been dedicated to the issues addressed in these materials, and their previous efforts provided the foundation on which this work was built. A national advisory committee to the project gave more time and expertise than was ever expected through active participation in all phases of the work.

Hundreds of volunteer NASW members contributed through six chapter-based project centers in 11 states. The Council on Social Work Education (CSWE) was a collaborating organization in this project, with dedicated members of the International Commission making valuable contributions. We extend a special thanks to Sally Van der Straeten and Yvonne Asamoah. Although it is impossible to name everyone who contributed, individuals from the project centers and the CSWE Curriculum Development Working Group deserve special recognition: Joe Gallegos, Marie Hoff, Janet Kusyk, Jennifer Stucker, and Daniel Tovar (Northwest Center on Violence, Development, and Ethnicity); Marilynn Moch and Beth S. Rosenthal (New York City NASW chapter Center on Violence, Development, and Poverty); Gerald Gray, Arleen B. Kahn, Mary Mussell, Arline Prigoff, and Krishna Samantrai (California NASW chapter Center on Violence, Development, and Trauma); Charles Figley, Kenneth Kazmerski, and Linda Vinton (Florida NASW chapter Center on Violence, Development, and Trauma); Bruce Ellsworth, Allie Kilpatrick, Pat Leahan, Rosemary Link, Rosemarie Merrigan, and Maura Sullivan (Minnesota NASW chapter Center on Violence, Development, and Women and Children); Shantha Balaswamy, James O. Billups, Lorraine Blackman, Debbie Ruboyianes, JoAnne St. Clair, Judy Smith, Chathapuram Ramanthan, and Jack Wall (Midwest Center on Violence, Development, and Substance Abuse).

The Alliance for a Global Community/InterAction provided critical information and expertise all along the way, always with a generous and enthusiastic response. A special thanks to Janet Green.

This project was funded in part by the U.S. Agency for International Development. Without their support, and that of their dedicated program officers, this project would not have happened. To Susan Saragi, in particular, thanks for helping us with all the details, large and small. David Watson and Elise Storck served as outstanding project officers, providing guidance and support at all phases of our work.

Lucy Sanchez was there from the beginning—helping to develop the grant proposal and shaping the project design. She continued to be at the forefront of the project through all its phases.

As national outreach coordinator, Bob Lagoyda provided an undying commitment and endless good ideas. John Rice gave heart and soul to the project as a social work intern at the NASW national office.

Gratitude goes to Brenda Ruiz-Bustos and Esperanca Cardoso for all the work they have done to ensure the success of the project and these materials.

Special thanks to Cheryl White for her hard work as a contributing editor for the briefing papers that formed the basis for the *Educational Resource*. Special thanks also to the development education consultants from the Development Studies Program for sharing their expertise with us: Margee Ensign, Ken Kusterer, and Sam Samarasinghe.

David Weiner and Paul Aaron of the Benton Foundation have been true partners in this endeavor and their guidance has been invaluable. The mission of the Benton Foundation is to strengthen the communications capacities of nonprofit organizations.

Linda Beebe, associate executive director, communications, at NASW, was instrumental in organizing these guides. Nancy Winchester, editorial services director, expedited the production process. Freelance editors Wendy Almeleh and

Louise Goines edited and refined the text. To all of them, our thanks.

And finally, our greatest appreciation to Eileen Kelly, who founded the Peace and International Affairs Program at NASW nine years ago. Her unending good humor has made this adventure a joy.

Jane Crosby and Dorothy Van Soest

PART I

MAKING THE CONNECTIONS BETWEEN VIOLENCE AND DEVELOPMENT

From the Los Angeles teenager whose friend is shot dead to the New York City executive who is mugged on a street corner, from the infant in Bombay who suffers from hunger to the poor farmer fleeing civil war in Rwanda, violence affects millions of people worldwide. With the evolution of sophisticated communication and transportation technologies, the world has become smaller and more interdependent. The global village—once just an abstract idea—is now a reality. Just as technology crosses borders, so do violence and related problems of concern to social workers, such as poverty and unemployment; the use and production of and trafficking in illegal drugs; discrimination; and the oppression of women and children. Increasingly, leaders and citizens are coming to understand that these problems can be solved not by the United States in isolation but by a world community working together. Social workers have a key role to play in this evolving effort.

KEY CONCEPTS

Sustainable Human Development

The term *development* may be defined as "meeting the basic needs of all and extending to all the opportunity to fulfill their aspirations for a better life" (Shuman, 1994, p. 2). According to this broad definition, development focuses on fostering economic opportunity, equity, human rights, dignity, democracy, peace, and spiritual and emotional well-being (Shuman & Harvey, 1993).

Social workers will readily understand this concept, for it is what they strive to do every day in their work with individuals, families, communities, and organizations. This resource will examine development from a national and international perspective.

Beginning in the late 1980s, a new consensus emerged within the international development community (see page 2) about the best means for achieving long-lasting, positive change in poor countries. The agreed-upon strategy, known as *sustainable human development*, is based on these underlying principles:
- meeting basic human needs for food, clean water, shelter, health care, and education
- expanding economic opportunities for people, especially poor people, to increase their productivity and earning capacity in ways that are environmentally, economically, and socially viable over the long term
- protecting the environment by managing natural resources in ways that take into account the needs of current and future generations
- promoting democratic participation, especially by poor women and men, in economic and political decisions that affect their lives
- encouraging adherence to internationally recognized human rights standards (*At the Crossroads*, 1995).

Global North, Global South

The term *global North* refers to the world's industrialized, wealthy countries, and the term *global South* refers to the world's poor nations. These terms are merely descriptive because the split between rich and poor nations does not fall along strict geographic lines. Social workers in the

The United States spent approximately 1 percent of its annual national budget, or $18 billion, on foreign assistance in 1996. Of this amount, 18 percent, or $3.2 billion, went to fund projects to help people in poor countries better their lives. Other money went toward military and security aid; food, exports, and other economic aid; and operating expenses (*Congressional Quarterly*, 1996).

In addition to federal funds, there are several hundred U.S.-based charitable international development organizations, called private voluntary organizations or nongovernmental organizations. These organizations receive an estimated $4.5 billion a year from individuals and businesses that is used to support relief and development efforts in the poorest nations of the world. Some of the better known organizations are Save the Children, CARE, Oxfam, and the American Red Cross (*Just 1%*, 1995).

United States have traditionally been concerned about poor communities that are hidden in urban centers or in isolated rural areas of this rich nation. Underdeveloped areas of the United States and countries of the global South share many characteristics, such as low standards of living, malnutrition, disease, illiteracy, unemployment, and the lack of adequate medical services.

According to figures on the per capita gross national products of countries throughout the world (World Bank, 1995), there are 24 high-income countries, with 15 percent of the world's people, including the United States, Switzerland, and Japan. Sixty-three countries, containing 29 percent of the world's population, such as the Philippines, Romania, and Iran, make up the middle-income category. And 45 countries, consisting of 56 percent of the world's population, including Guatemala, Somalia, and Bangladesh, constitute the low-income sector.

The global South is where

- about 77 percent of the world's population lives

- almost a billion people live in dire poverty
- about half the people do not know how to read
- a billion people in the labor force are unemployed or underemployed
- typically, the top 20 percent of the population receives 50 percent of the income, and the bottom 20 percent receives less than 5 percent of the income
- 75 percent of rural people do not have access to clean drinking water
- more than half a billion people are hungry and malnourished
- almost 20 percent of the children die before the age of five
- 100 million children are always hungry
- 15 million children die each year from a combination of malnutrition and infection
- the average life expectancy is 54 years compared with 74 years in the global North (Kerschner, 1992; United Nations Children's Fund, 1994).

Violence

Violence may be broadly defined as an act or situation that harms the health or well-being of oneself or others. It includes both direct attacks on a person's physical and psychological integrity and destructive acts that do not involve a direct relationship between victims and the institution or person or persons responsible for the harm (Bulhan, 1985).

One goal of the Violence and Development Project is to expand the common perception of violence to include such problems as racism, sexism, poverty, and hunger. These social ills grow out of institutions, governments, and economic structures that encourage the domination of certain groups of people over other groups and perpetuate unequal access to wealth and other resources. Inequities, which may be based on class, race, gender, or ethnicity, are often enforced by the use of violence by police forces, government troops or their proxies, foreign powers, and other forms of sanctioned militarism.

Threats to personal security and social stability come from several sources (see Table 1). These sources include social and economic systems (deprivation, lack of access, and oppression), the state (repression, torture, and police brutality or inaction), other countries (colonization and war), other groups of people (civil war, ethnic conflict, discrimination, and hate crimes), and individuals or gangs (homicide and muggings). Violence may be directed against specific groups, such as women (rape, domestic violence, and lack of access to higher education or better-paying jobs), children (child abuse and neglect), and ethnic populations (genocide, hate crimes, and discrimination) or against the self (suicide and substance abuse). Among the underlying principles of the Violence and Development Project is that long-term solutions to violence must include permanent changes in structural and institutional systems that give rise to deprivation and oppression and create a world of haves and have-nots.

IN TODAY'S WORLD, INEQUITIES ABOUND

Although more than three-fourths of the world's 5.8 billion people live in the global South, they enjoy only 16 percent of the world's income (UN Development Programme, 1995). One person in four in the global South is unable to satisfy such basic needs as adequate nutrition, safe and sufficient drinking water, clean air to breathe, proper sanitation, and access to health care and elementary education (Sivard, 1993).

Development efforts to address social problems are also needed in the United States. Although this is the richest, most powerful nation in the world, poverty and inequity stubbornly persist. For all its resources, the United States ranks 21st among 132 countries in infant mortality (World Bank, 1995). And despite this country's system of free public education through the secondary level, 50 percent of adults who took part in a nationwide literacy survey scored in the lowest two levels of proficiency, placing them in an at-risk category for low earnings and limited choices for employment (Kirsch, Jungeblut, Jenkins, & Kolstad, 1993). These examples underscore the point that wealth is not necessarily synonymous with greater development.

The common perception is that the global South is fraught with destitution and despair. Yet since 1960, development assistance has helped reduce infant mortality rates in developing countries by 50 percent, increase life expectancy from 46 years to 63 years, and increase primary school enrollment from 48 percent to 78 percent (*Just 1%*, 1995). In some cases, development achievements in poor countries have surpassed those of richer nations. For example, in Honduras, 92 percent of the children under age two are immunized, whereas in Detroit, the rate is 28 percent (Alliance for a Global Community, 1994a). U.S. social workers can learn a great deal from people in the global South who have established

TABLE 1. SOURCES OF THREATS TO PERSONAL SECURITY AND SOCIAL STABILITY

Structural	Institutional	Personal
Avoidable deprivations built into the structure of society based on norms and traditions that subjugate one group in favor of another (poverty, hunger)	Harmful acts by organizations and institutions (oppression, unequal treatment under the law, police brutality, torture)	Interpersonal acts of violence against persons or property (rape, murder, muggings)
	Official forms of violence (state repression, war, and invasion)	Harmful acts against self (alcohol abuse, drug abuse, suicide)
		Acts by organized groups or mobs (hate crimes, looting, rioting)

programs to improve social and economic development in their communities and who understand the need for bettering social institutions as well as individuals.

VIOLENCE AND DEVELOPMENT: MAKING THE CONNECTION

Violence and poverty obstruct the development of human capital—the term used by economists to describe a nation's collective ideas, labor, knowledge, and problem-solving skills. Nations find it difficult or impossible to take care of their own—let alone compete in the international marketplace—when they are burdened with widespread hunger, unemployment, or war. The famine in Somalia that gripped the world's attention in 1992 was the direct result of civil war. The conflict prevented people from planting their crops—food on which they depended to survive.

People continue to fight wars around the world, eating up precious resources that could be used for human development. In 1993, countries in the global South spent as much on military power as the poorest 2 billion people on earth earned in total income (Sivard, 1993). Furthermore, the United States spent $291 billion on military expenditures in 1993—seven times the amount spent by Japan, the country with the next largest military budget (*U.S. Military Spending*, 1993)—and U.S. spending is still on the rise (Hartung, 1994). Thus, in both poor and wealthy countries, military spending drains resources from social programs, widening the disparities between the rich and the poor (Iatridis, 1988; Korotkin, 1985; Sivard, 1993).

REDUCING VIOLENCE THROUGH SUSTAINABLE HUMAN DEVELOPMENT

Examples of successful development projects abound, demonstrating that progress can be made when there is a commitment to developing human potential and the leadership to carry out that commitment. Some projects have been initiated by governments that are serious about alleviating social problems; others have been spearheaded by a single individual with a driving vision.

The Grameen Bank, founded by economics professor Muhammad Yunus in Bangladesh in 1976, is an example of a cost-effective development initiative that has changed the world. From 1976 to 1994, the bank lent over $1 billion to 2 million people and, in the process, created jobs and supported small businesses (Alliance for a Global Community, 1994b). Nearly half the borrowers have lifted themselves out of poverty.

So successful was Yunus's vision for the poor that his concept of "microenterprise" has been emulated by governments, community groups, and private organizations in Central and South America, Asia, Africa, and the United States. By making small loans (usually less than $100), community-run lending programs enable poor people to boost their earning power, gain greater independence, and better provide for themselves and their children. And with worldwide repayment rates of over 95 percent, such programs have proved that, with support, people can indeed overcome poverty (Alliance for a Global Community, 1994b).

IMPLICATIONS FOR SOCIAL WORKERS

The future of the United States is intertwined with the futures of the nations of the global South. Social work support for human and economic development efforts around the world makes sense as part of an overall program for addressing domestic concerns. Here are a few examples:

1. Global disparities in wealth contribute to political instability and wars, resulting in an influx of refugees and immigrants into the United States. Other nations' wars also affect the United States by limiting the economic growth of its trade partners, by threatening the security of the country's borders and those of its allies, and by causing environmental degradation that crosses national boundaries.
2. Poverty tempts farmers in the global South to engage in the production of illegal drugs, while social workers combat the effects of drug use in this country.

3. Poverty and hunger give poor workers in the global South no choice but to accept jobs with extremely low wages and poor working conditions, with the result that U.S. companies move many of their operations to these countries to take advantage of cheap labor and jobs flow out of the United States. Meanwhile, social workers in this country struggle with the effects of unemployment and increased prejudice and discrimination against immigrants and racial and ethnic groups that is born out of a desire to blame someone for the country's diminishing real incomes.

Social work's ethic of care requires that there be no distinction between "our" poor and "their" poor. The social justice tradition of the profession provides a moral justification for working toward a time when all people will share the world's wealth. Giving poor people access to resources aimed at improving their health, education, and economic status enhances their capability to lead more fulfilling lives and to improve the lot of their children, both of which have lasting implications for the future.

U.S. social workers are uniquely positioned to participate in the international effort to promote global security and development because they have the following capabilities:

- They know how to develop and implement successful interventions to alleviate social problems. In addition, they are trained to consider a problem at the individual, family, community, organizational, and national levels, and the future points toward the inclusion of an international perspective as well.

- They understand the connection between a client's well-being and the political, social, and economic context within which the client lives.

- They adhere to principles that mirror those of successful development, including addressing the basic unmet needs of people first, listening to people and helping them define their own needs, empowering people to make their own decisions, promoting leadership skills, and encouraging democratic participation.

- They have expertise in issues of inner-city development—issues that will be more and more essential as the global South becomes increasingly urbanized.

WHAT YOU CAN DO

Here are some ways in which you can help address problems related to violence and development:

- Learn more about nations of the global South and this country's relationship to them, using the references and resources presented at the end of Part 1 as a start. Talk to people from the countries of the global South who are in the United States. Join a study or travel group.

- Educate yourself about U.S. foreign aid by reading a variety of sources. Support foreign assistance aimed at sustainable human development.

- Learn about, support, and participate in international events, such as the World Summit for Social Development and the World Summit on Children.

- Join organizations that are committed to gun control and reducing violence with the use of guns.

- Learn conflict-resolution strategies as an alternative to violence.

- Teach your children and your young clients respect for people from other countries and cultures. Explain that physical aggression is not the smart way to solve problems and educate them about the consequences of violence.

REFERENCES

Alliance for a Global Community. (1994a). How they compare: Immunization in the U.S. and the developing world. *Connections, 1*(3).

Alliance for a Global Community. (1994b). Micro-enterprise: Small loans, big returns. *Connections, 1*(2).

At the crossroads: The future of foreign aid (Occasional Paper No. 4). (1995). (Available from Bread for the World Institute, 1100 Wayne Avenue, Suite 1000, Silver Spring, MD 20910; phone 301-608-2400)

Bulhan, H. A. (1985). *Frantz Fanon and the psychology of oppression*. New York: Plenum Press.

Congressional Quarterly. (1996, June 1). Weekly report.

Hartung, W. D. (1994). *And weapons for all*. New York: HarperCollins.

Iatridis, D. S. (1988). New social deficit: Neoconservatism's policy of social underdevelopment. *Social Work, 33*, 11–15.

Just 1% (1995). (Brochure available from InterAction, 1717 Massachusetts Avenue, NW, Suite 801, Washington, DC 20036; phone 202-667-8227)

Kerschner, H. K. (1992). *An organizing guide for community-based education and international action*. Washington, DC: American Association for International Aging.

Kirsch, I. S., Jungeblut, A., Jenkins, L., & Kolstad, A. (1993). *Adult literacy in America*. Washington, DC: National Center for Education Statistics.

Korotkin, A. (1985). Impact of military spending on the nation's quality of life. *Social Work, 30*, 369–372.

Shuman, M. (1994). *Toward a global village: International community development initiatives*. Boulder, CO: Pluto Press.

Shuman, M., & Harvey, H. (1993). *Security without war: A post–cold war foreign policy*. Boulder, CO: Westview Press.

Sivard, R. L. (1993). *World military and social expenditures 1993*. Washington, DC: World Priorities.

United Nations Children's Fund. (1994). *The state of the world's children, 1994*. New York: Oxford University Press.

United Nations Development Programme. (1995). *Human development report, 1995*. New York: Oxford University Press.

U.S. military spending: In a league of its own. (1993). (Available from Campaign for New Priorities, 424 C Street, NE, Washington, DC 20002; phone 202-544-8226)

World Bank. (1995). *World Development Report 1995*. New York: Oxford University Press.

ADDITIONAL RESOURCES

Organizations

Alliance for a Global Community
1717 Massachusetts Avenue, NW, Suite 801
Washington, DC 20036
Phone: 202-667-8227

An organization that publishes *Connections*, a newsletter, 10 times a year, with information about the connections between the United States and developing countries.

Brookings Institute
1775 Massachusetts Avenue, NW
Washington, DC 20036
Phone: 202-797-6105

An organization that is engaged in research, education, and publications on important issues of foreign and domestic policy. Publishes the quarterly *Brookings Review*, as well as a variety of books.

Global Exchange
2017 Mission Street, Suite 303
San Francisco, CA 94110
Phone: 415-255-7296 or 1-800-497-1994

An organization that sponsors reality tours and study seminars to Africa, Asia, Latin America, and the Caribbean and publishes books on international issues.

InterAction: American Council for Voluntary International Action
1717 Massachusetts Avenue, NW, Suite 801
Washington, DC 20036
Phone: 202-667-8227

An umbrella organization for several hundred international development agencies with programs throughout the world.

International Activities Committee
Office of Peace and International Affairs
National Association of Social Workers
750 First Street, NE, Suite 700
Washington, DC 20002-4241
Phone: 202-336-8388
or 1-800-638-8799

An NASW committee that oversees and coordinates educational and other programs related to international issues and social work and disseminates a newsletter to NASW members who ask to be placed on the international network.

United Nations Department of Public Information
United Nations, Room S-1040
New York, NY 10017
Phone: 212-963-4475

The department publishes a series of issue papers on topics related to world development, such as the family, human rights, and women, from various UN conferences, for example, the United Nations World Summit for Social Development held in March 1995.

Reports

Human Development Report. Produced by the UN Development Programme (phone 1-800-253-9646) and published annually by Oxford University Press.

Hunger 1995: The Causes of Hunger. Published by Bread for the World Institute (1100 Wayne Avenue, Suite 1000, Silver Spring, MD 20910; phone 301-608-2400).

The State of the World's Children. Produced by the UN Children's Fund and published annually by Oxford University Press. Available at bookstores or from the U.S. Committee for UNICEF (phone 212-686-5522).

World Development Report. Produced by the World Bank and published annually by Oxford University Press (available from the World Bank Bookstore: phone 202-473-2941).

World Military and Social Expenditures. By Ruth Sivard. Published periodically (every three or so years) by and available from World Priorities (phone 202-965-1661).

PART 2

POVERTY

ENSURING ENOUGH FOR EVERYONE

Everyone has the right to a standard of living adequate for the health and well-being of himself and his family, including food, clothing, housing and medical care, and necessary social services.

—Universal Declaration of Human Rights,
Article 25

Poverty anywhere is a threat to prosperity everywhere.

—Human Development Report, 1993

Over the past 50 years, many gains have been made in raising the standard of living for people around the globe. Nevertheless, poverty remains ubiquitous:

- One-fifth of all human beings live in absolute poverty, without adequate food, clothing, and shelter (United Nations [UN], 1995c).
- Fifteen percent of people in the United States—one of the most affluent countries in the world—live below the poverty line (UN Development Programme, 1994).
- In the global South, about 1.3 billion people (almost one-third of the population) live below the poverty line. Nearly 800 million people do not get enough food (UN Development Programme, 1995).

In spite of efforts to close the gap between the rich and the poor, inequities persist. Between 1960 and 1991, the share of the world's income for the richest 20 percent of the global population increased from 70 percent to 85 percent. During the same period, the already meager share of the world's income for the poorest 20 percent of the global population decreased from 2.3 percent to 1.4 percent (UN Development Programme, 1994). Discrepancies between the wealth of the global North and the global South are equally striking. Wealthy nations in general have almost tripled their per capita incomes since 1950. In contrast, the per capita incomes in the poorest countries—home to 77 percent of the world's population—have stagnated (Epstein, Graham, & Nemhard, 1993).

Poverty and inequity are passive forms of violence that impede human development (New York City NASW chapter Center, 1994). Mahatma Gandhi characterized poverty as the worst form of violence (Dasgupta, 1968). Part 2 examines the conditions and consequences of poverty, both at home and abroad. It discusses the connections between poverty, violence, and development and considers some initiatives that have been designed to break the poverty trap.

POVERTY DEFINED

Absolute poverty refers to the inability to obtain the goods and services needed to meet socially defined minimum needs. In the United States, the official government measure of absolute poverty is based on the minimum annual amount of money required to sustain a family ($14,335 for a family of four in 1992) (DiNitto, 1995, p. 69).

According to the definition of *relative poverty*, a person is poor when his or her income is significantly less than the average income of the general population. This definition focuses on inequality of incomes, rather than the absence of resources to provide for absolute needs (Schiller, 1989).

WHAT CAUSES POVERTY?

Despite the historic tendency to blame poor people for their problems, the vast majority of people do not choose to be poor. Rather, throughout the world, poverty is a result of many factors, among them:

- lack of access to economic "building blocks," such as land, seeds, water, tools, training, and education
- unemployment or underemployment
- inequitable distribution of global resources, including food
- inadequate government support for needed social supports
- discrimination against ethnic and racial groups and women, who are disproportionately represented among poor people
- war and military spending, which drain limited resources that could be used for human development.

There are considerable differences between the poverty conditions faced by people in the industrialized global North and the mass poverty experienced by people in the global South. But poor people worldwide have one thing in common: They do not receive sufficient support. Many people have an inflated idea of how much help the U.S. government is giving poor people. This perception was reflected in a 1995 survey of 1,200 U.S. voters, 19 percent of whom cited welfare as the biggest item in the federal budget and 27 percent of whom cited foreign aid. In reality, welfare was only 1.1 percent of the federal budget in 1995, and foreign aid was even less than that (*U.S. Budget for FY '97*, 1996).

POVERTY, VIOLENCE, AND DEVELOPMENT: MAKING CONNECTIONS

Poverty is violence—violence against people. Physical, mental, psychological, intellectual, emotional, social, legal, political, you-name-it violence. It is ugly and angry and everywhere.

—Lourie, 1968, p. 1

Poverty Affects Human Health

Worldwide, threats to health are typically greater for the poorest people, particularly children in rural areas. In the global South, an estimated 17 million people die from infectious and parasitic diseases each year. Most of these deaths are linked with poor nutrition and unsafe living conditions, including polluted water (UN Development Programme, 1994).

Statistics on health care are also bleak. There is but one physician for every 7,000 people in the global South versus one physician for every 400 people in the more prosperous global North. Yet, even though people in the global North are more likely to have access to health care than are people elsewhere, 40 million low-income Americans still did not have health insurance in 1996—up from 35 million in 1989 and 37 million in 1993 (UN Development Programme, 1994; Wines & Pear, 1996).

Poverty Impedes Child Development

According to the UN (1995a), in the global South,

- about 13 million children under age five die each year from easily preventable diseases and malnutrition
- an estimated 130 million children, almost two-thirds of them girls, lack access to primary education
- an estimated 200 million youngsters are forced to work for their own or their families' survival, often under dangerous and exploitative conditions.

Poverty takes its toll on children in the United States as well:

> Across an astonishing range of outcomes—including premature death, stunted growth, physical impairment, injury, learning disability, low educational achievement, school failure, abuse and neglect, extreme behavioral problems, and delinquency—poor children fare worse than children who grow up in families that are able to meet their basic needs. (Sherman, 1994, p. 16)

Poverty Breeds Shame, Fear, and Anger

Economic hardship contributes to parental stress and depression. Case study 1, of Anne and Susan, is one mother's account of the horrible effects of poverty on her and her daughter.

CASE STUDY 1
Anne and Susan

> Susan was raised in poverty and I am still learning the many ways it hurt her. I [Anne] am her mother. Susan was born two weeks after my 18th birthday and by the time she was 12, we had moved more than 30 times, always one step ahead of or behind the eviction notices, gas and light disconnect notices, and various other bills haunting our mailbox. We laughed a lot and tried to make it an adventure, like the time she was six and the two of us had to move our bed across town on a bus.
>
> But then I would cry and cry for days at a time. Being poor made me crazy, and Susan learned to be my support, caretaker, and defender before she could read.
>
> A few times I tried to kill myself out of fear and shame at not being able to keep a roof over our heads, out of anger over not being able to keep a job and needing to return over and over again to welfare, out of desperation whenever the welfare department would cut off my eligibility by mistake.
>
> Poverty was more than not having enough. It was about not having any control over the most intimate parts of our lives, and, for me, about feeling shame, fear, and anger all the time. After more than 20 low-wage jobs, I enrolled in college when Susan was eight. A few years later, we received a rent subsidy which allowed us to stay in one place. Things got a bit better. For the first time in either of our lives, we had [a] community, permanent friends, and a sense of belonging. Today, Susan and I are successful professionals, and best friends. It didn't take much: a rent subsidy, a generous state university admissions policy, and access to mental health services. The rest we did on our own (From *Wasting America's Future* by Arloe Sherman, ©1994 by Children's Defense Fund, reprinted by permission of Beacon Press, Boston, p. 30).

Poverty Contributes to Violence

Juvenile crime and violence are highly correlated with poverty and other factors related to underdevelopment, including unemployment and inadequate education and social services (UN Development Programme, 1994). The same holds true for adult crime and violence. "Despite some findings to the contrary, a significant correlation has been shown to exist among societal inequality, discrimination, and homicide. Among all groups in the U.S., regardless of race, homicide is found disproportionately among the lowest socioeconomic groups" (Hawkins, 1990, p. 160). In Washington, DC, for example, the poorest part of the city has a violent crime rate 13 times higher than the wealthiest part (Sherman, 1994).

Poverty and inequity set the stage for ethnic conflict as well. Contrary to widespread belief, violence does not spring naturally from ethnic differences:

> Modern states . . . create an economic barrier between mainstream populations—the rich and the educated—and ethnic populations—the poor and the marginalized. The ensuing power struggles generate the sorts of violent civil conflict that many observers attribute to some sort of natural hostility. But [different ethnic groups]

are not predetermined enemies, and when these peoples have adequate space and autonomy, their basic capacity for respect and problem-solving will flourish. (Boulding, 1995, p. 9)

Inadequate and Ineffective Development Contribute to Poverty

In the 1950s and 1960s, several nations in the global South implemented ambitious development programs using Western technology and aid. Because of poor planning, many of these programs served only to marginalize struggling people further. When mechanized farm technology, designed to increase crop yields, was introduced in Iran, for example, scores of laborers were no longer needed. These laborers were forced to migrate to overcrowded cities, where they found little work or other services (Rohr, 1989).

In poor countries, industrial initiatives that are motivated solely by the desire for profits and that confer value on individuals only to the extent that they produce profits merely exploit the very people who should benefit from them (UN Development Programme, 1994). Case study 2, of Randy Conway and Angelica Hernandez, highlights the negative effects of unjust development on two families, one in the United States, the other in the global South.

CASE STUDY 2
Randy Conway and Angelica Hernandez

Randy Conway is 44 years old and lives with his wife and three children in the small town of Mount Vernon, Missouri. He worked 20 years in a Zenith factory making televisions. Zenith had moved from the northern United States to Missouri in 1976, in search of workers who were willing to toil for lower wages and without the benefit of trade unions. By 1992, Randy was making $11 per hour, but then Zenith moved 20,000 of its U.S. jobs to Mexico, including most of the jobs in Missouri. Randy is now out of work. Zenith spokesman John Taylor admitted that "the wage structure in Mexico is a primary reason for our relocation there."

Angelica Hernandez has worked in Zenith's Reynosa, Mexico, factory since 1988. She works in a noisy plant with hazardous chemicals all around and takes home $35 for a 48-hour week. Angelica, her husband, and their seven children live in a dirt-floor shack, 12 feet by 18 feet, that has no electricity and no running water (*GATT and NAFTA*, n.d.).

Summarizing the North–South Poverty Link

The global North and the global South are linked in several ways:
1. Keeping wages suppressed in the global South causes companies to relocate jobs from high-wage countries like the United States to developing countries. The result: unemployment at home and exploitation of workers in the global South.
2. Poverty in the global South forces people to migrate to prosperous countries in search of jobs and other opportunities. Immigrants often face racism and ethnic violence in their adopted countries, particularly when they settle in financially stretched communities. Many families are separated in the process of migrating. Consequently, newcomers are further isolated.
3. Countries that are desperate to pay off their debts pillage their natural resources to gain new income, and their actions promote global warming and water pollution (Danaher, 1994).

ALLEVIATING POVERTY THROUGH SUSTAINABLE HUMAN DEVELOPMENT

Three interrelated strategies—reducing poverty, creating employment, and increasing social integration—are at the core of sustainable human development. These strategies are consistent with principles embodied in the Universal Declaration of Human Rights (UN, 1985).

The UN Development Programme (1994) recommended that countries pursue the following measures to alleviate poverty:
* provide poor people with access to basic services, such as health care, housing, and clean water

- invest in education, training, and skills development, especially for women
- ensure equal access to land, agricultural resources, credit, and information
- involve poor people in the design of poverty-reduction strategies
- create a market environment that facilitates new employment opportunities
- guarantee basic legal rights to all
- implement antidiscrimination measures and apply stiff penalties for violations
- support grassroots organizations that provide citizens with direct participation in decision making.

Communities Mobilize to Tackle Poverty

Change is occurring in local communities around the world as women's groups, peasant groups, religious organizations, consumer advocates, and environmental protection societies work to break the poverty trap (Breslin, 1995). Case study 3, of Wangari Maathai, describes how the actions of one individual can evolve into a communitywide development initiative that empowers people to reduce poverty.

CASE STUDY 3
Wangari Maathai

In 1977, Wangari Maathai went into her backyard in Kenya and planted seven small trees. "I realized that when you talk about the problems, you tend to make people feel that there is nothing they can do. To break that cycle, one has to start with a positive step. Planting a tree is very simple—something positive that anybody can do."

As a member of the National Council of Women of Kenya, Maathai enlisted some women farmers to plant more trees. In the beginning, Mobil Oil Corporation provided funding for tree nurseries. Now the funding comes from nonprofit organizations and in the form of small donations from women all over the world. The nurseries that supply the indigenous trees are located in rural areas where they provide jobs for local people who then train other local people how to grow and plant them.

People not only get the benefit of the trees and earn a living but take responsibility for their environment and themselves. The Green Belt movement has also grown to include training for women in nutrition and family planning and has expanded its agenda to challenge oppressive social institutions.

As Maathai put it, "The Green Belt Movement is a movement to empower people, to raise their consciousness, to give them hope. It shows them that the power to change their environment is within themselves, and within their own capacities" (Maathai, 1988, p. 1).

Role of Nongovernmental Organizations

Thousands of nongovernmental organizations (NGOs) around the world are playing an important role in addressing poverty and related problems through empowering citizens and engaging in international advocacy for the rights of marginalized people. Vital lessons can be learned from the development approaches of NGOs that encourage communities to take control of their futures (UN, 1995b). In Tanzania, for example, the Community Development Trust Fund helped members of a poor village establish their own health clinic and encouraged residents' participation in all phases of the project (Ngaiza, 1989).

Grassroots Economic Alternatives

A new wave of grassroots organizations in the global South and the United States are redefining economic development to incorporate principles of equity, democratic participation, and environmental sustainability (GATT and NAFTA, n.d.) using two strategies: cooperatives and revolving credit.

- Cooperatives. In countries as diverse as Zimbabwe and Mexico, family farmers have formed cooperatives to produce and market their products. In the mountains of Mexico's Guerrero province, for example, campesinos have organized a regional alliance of cooperatives to manage their coffee and honey exports (GATT and NAFTA, n.d.).
- Revolving credit. Most of the world's poor people suffer from the lack of access to credit.

Many groups have been pooling and lending capital to the poor to enable them to start small businesses or to improve farming practices (*GATT and NAFTA*, n.d.).

Case studies 4 and 5 present examples of how poor people in the global South have improved their lives through grassroots efforts.

CASE STUDY 4
A Bank for Poor People

In 1976, Muhammad Yunus, a professor-turned-banker, offered tiny loans to the poorest people in one village in Bangladesh. The people proved to be good at using the money to earn income and at paying back the loans. Although the poor borrowers were honest and hardworking, conventional bankers did not choose to see them as such and would not give them loans.

Because of the encouraging results of Yunus's initial loan program, the program was expanded to two villages, then to 10 villages, to one district and then to five districts in Bangladesh. Throughout the process, conventional bankers kept saying, "What you are seeing is not the real thing. The real thing is that the poor have no will to work, they have no ability. They will never return your money" (Yunus, 1994, p. xi). However, people continued to pay back the money, and the program kept expanding. As Yunus (1994) noted:

> Today, Grameen Bank, the poor people's bank in Bangladesh, operates in 34,000 villages, exactly half the number of all the villages in Bangladesh. Grameen Bank currently lends money to 1.7 million borrowers, 94% of whom are women. The borrowers own the bank. We lend out over $30 million each month in loans averaging less than $100. The repayment rate for our loans is over 98%. Besides income-generating loans, we also give housing loans. A typical housing loan is $300. We have given more than 220,000 housing loans so far with a perfect repayment record. Studies done on Grameen tell us that the borrowers have improved their income, widened their asset base and moved steadily toward crossing the poverty line and toward a life of dignity and honor. Studies also tell us that in Grameen families the nutrition level is better than in non-Grameen families, child mortality is lower and adoption of family-planning practices is higher. All studies confirm the visible empowerment of women. (p. xi)

The Grameen Bank is different from other banks in many ways. For example, to build commitment and provide community support, a prospective client must find five friends to borrow with. Considerable time is spent preparing the five-member group to learn how to make decisions and to operate as a community. For instance, questions are raised with the group about their reactions if one of them should fail to pay his or her weekly installment. The advice that is repeatedly given to the group is this:

> Please never get angry with the person who cannot pay the installment. Please don't put pressure on her to make her pay. Be a good friend, don't turn into an enemy. As a good friend, your first response should be, "Oh my God, she is in trouble, we must go and help her out." (Yunus, 1994, p. xii)

The Grameen Bank is based on the principle that the borrower knows best, and borrowers are encouraged to make their own decisions within the context of community and responsibility to each other. The money that is paid back by borrowers provides the resources for further loans, and the five-member group develops as a franchise.

CASE STUDY 5
What One Can Learn from India

The Self-Employed Women's Association (SEWA) holds to the simple yet radical belief that poor women need organizing, not welfare. Based in a dusty old textile town called Ahmedabad on the edge of a desert, SEWA is a trade union for self-employed people. It offers union membership to people such as the illiterate women who sell vegetables for 50 cents a day in the city markets or who pick up paper scraps for recycling from the streets.

When a woman joins SEWA, her income increases because the power of the union allows her to obtain better prices from the middlemen who supply her vegetables or who purchase her scraps of paper. Then she puts the extra income toward her family's education and health care or birth control. The oppressed Indian woman also begins to change the way she thinks of herself when she joins SEWA. She starts to see herself as a worker, an active producer—not just someone's wife or daughter-in-law. When her self-image begins to change, she meets women from other communities, and the barriers of caste begin to break down.

SEWA has a membership of 150,000 women, the vast majority of whom are poor and illiterate. It has organized women into 70 different trade cooperatives, from fish vending to cattle raising to weaving to hand rolling small Indian cigarettes. SEWA now provides health care and insurance for its members. In addition, SEWA continues to expand, with its reputation growing well beyond the borders of India.

What does all this mean for the United States? At a time when the United States seems intent on ending welfare as it now exists, SEWA may provide a model. From the dust bowls of India to the South Bronx of New York City, a simple truth has emerged: Give people some control over their destinies and watch as a spirit of enterprise emerges. Another truth that has become apparent around the world is that women are the real agents for change, both in the United States and in the global South.

Credit for All

Study after study on credit schemes for poor people has confirmed that poor people are credit worthy:

- Poor people can save, even if only a little.
- Poor people are reliable borrowers. Repayment rates of 90 percent and more are not rare.
- Poor people are able and willing to pay market interest rates, so that credit schemes for poor people stand a good chance of becoming viable, self-financing undertakings.
- Credit schemes for poor people work because they significantly improve people's incomes—typically by more than 20 percent and, at times, by more than 100 percent (UN Development Programme, 1994).

MYTHS ABOUT HUNGER

Myth: People are hungry because there is not enough food in the world. If poor people stopped having so many children, there would be enough food for everyone.

Reality: Rapid population growth is an important contributor to world hunger. However, the inequitable distribution of resources and the overconsumption of resources by affluent people are equally significant causes. The world produces enough food for everyone to have 2,500 calories a day—150 more than the basic minimum—if food is distributed and consumed equally. Although wealthy people, mostly in industrialized countries, make up only 20 percent of the world's population, they control 85 percent of its income and consume 80 percent of its resources (*Hunger 1995,* 1995).

Myth: Hunger is not a problem in the United States.

Reality: In the United States, an estimated 30 million people cannot afford to buy enough food to maintain good health, and 12 million children under age 18 are hungry. In 1992, the last year for which information is available, 15 percent of U.S. residents—38 million people—lived below the poverty line and faced the threat of hunger (*Hunger 1995,* 1995).

Myth: There is not much of a connection between violence and hunger.

Reality: Hunger and poverty breed violence. People who live in an affluent society but cannot obtain the necessary income to feed, clothe, and house their families sometimes turn to violence, crime, and selling drugs as their only means of survival. In the United States, someone dies from a gunshot wound every 14 minutes. Acute-care hospitals in Washington, DC, spend more than $20 million a year treating injuries from violent crime. Moreover, the incidences of homicide and suicide are higher in low-income communities than in middle-class communities (*Hunger 1995,* 1995). To end the vicious cycle of violence in this country, hunger must be alleviated.

Myth: No one has to be hungry. All people can pull themselves up by their bootstraps.

Reality: Race, ethnicity, gender, and age all have a powerful impact on who is hungry and who eats. Structural-level violence ensures that the system of inequity continues even when people work hard to provide for their basic needs. Worldwide, racial and ethnic minorities and women lack equal access to resources, have fewer opportunities, and thus are less able to provide for themselves and more vulnerable to hunger (*Hunger 1995*, 1995).

MYTHS ABOUT POVERTY AND INTERNATIONAL DEVELOPMENT

Myth: The global South is composed of poor countries that are overwhelmingly dominated by poverty, violence, and human misery. The problems are so enormous that there is really nothing that anyone can do.

Reality: The countries of the global South have average annual per capita gross national products (GNPs) of less than $2,000 and are faced with problems related to poverty, hunger, overpopulation, education, health, environment, and debt (Kerschner, 1991). However, there is a widespread tendency to overestimate the needs of people in the global South and thus to feel hopeless and helpless in the face of what is perceived as enormous problems, as in the list of misperceptions (Kerschner, 1991) in the next column.

Myth: In spite of billions of dollars spent in foreign aid, conditions continue to be just as bad in the global South.

Reality: Conditions have greatly improved for people in the global South since 1950 as a result of four decades of assistance from the United States, other industrialized nations, and poor countries themselves. The record of human development is unprecedented, with the global South setting a pace three times faster than industrial countries did a century ago. Rising rates of life expectancy, falling rates of infant mortality, increasing educational attainment, and much improved nutrition are a few of the heartening indicators.

During the 1980s and continuing into the 1990s, social progress in many African and Latin American countries slowed down and, in some cases, retreated. Yet the immense progress made during the previous three decades illustrates the value of cooperative development. For example, it took only 35 years to lower the infant mortality rate in the global South from 200 per thousand to 70 per thousand live births, an achievement it took European countries a century to gain; be-tween 1950 and 1986, life expectancy increased from 37 to 61 years in low-income countries; by 1986, 60 percent of the population of the global South could read, compared with only 30 percent in 1950 (Kerschner, 1991; UN Development Programme, 1994). According to UNICEF (1994), 24 countries in the global South have already reduced malnutrition by 10 percent or more, and 30 of 61 other poor countries for which information was available were on track to reduce child malnutrition by 20 percent by 1995.

Misperception	Fact
Most of the world's children are starving.	1 percent to 2 percent of the world's children are visibly malnourished.
The vast majority of the world's families are living in absolute poverty.	20 percent to 25 percent of the world's families are poor.
Only 10 percent to 20 percent of the world's six- to 12-year-old children start school.	Almost 90 percent of the world's six- to 12-year-old children start school.
The rate of population growth in the global South is increasing.	The rate of population growth is decreasing in every region of the global South, including Africa.

Myth: The United States is the most generous foreign-assistance provider in the world.

Reality: The United States has dropped to fourth place behind Japan, France, and Germany in the amount it spends on foreign aid (in dollars). However, as a percentage of the GNP contributed, the United States is 21st, with foreign aid expenditures of less than 1 percent of federal outlays, compared to 15 percent during the Marshall Plan in the late 1940s (Kerschner, 1991; Lippmann, 1996).

Myth: Most disaster relief to the global South comes from industrialized nations in the global North.

Reality: Most disaster relief comes from the global South through efforts by indigenous people and organizations or from other poor countries.

Myth: Only a small percentage of U.S. trade is with poor countries.

Reality: Nine out of 10 countries that are leading importers of U.S. commodities, such as South Korea and Thailand, were once recipients of U.S. foreign assistance (Alliance for a Global Community, 1995). From 1985 to 1995, U.S. exports to developing countries more than doubled—from $71 billion to $180 billion. Every additional $1 billion in exported goods resulted in 20,000 new U.S. jobs (*Just 1%*, 1995).

Myth: Foreign assistance only helps other countries, the United States reaps no benefits from it, and it does not alleviate the problems in this country with which social workers are concerned.

Reality: It is important to understand how foreign assistance is linked to social problems in the United States. By helping countries in the global South to deal with and solve their problems, we Americans are inevitably helping ourselves and addressing our own problems. The following examples illustrate how foreign aid is not simply assistance to other countries but a form of social work intervention that addresses problems and assists clients in the United States through global cooperation.

- Foreign assistance can be seen as a social work intervention to combat unemployment and the decrease in the number of jobs in the United States caused by the movement of industries to developing countries. Many of the estimated billion people in the global South who live in absolute poverty are forced to work for little money in dangerous and extremely poor working conditions, which makes them attractive resources for corporate profits. They also have no money to buy U.S. products; in the 1980s, for instance, the United States lost 1.5 million to 2 million jobs because of diminished purchasing power in the developing world. As a result of economic and social development, workers in a more prosperous developing world could demand higher wages and decent working conditions and would have more money to spend on imported U.S. products, thereby creating jobs and reducing this country's trade deficit (Shuman, 1994).
- Foreign assistance can be seen as a preventive measure to address the large number of refugees who enter the United States with multiple problems as a result of having undergone tremendous suffering. Violence, oppression, and poverty in Africa, Asia, the Middle East, and Latin America have driven hundreds of thousands of people from their homelands to this country, presenting a new array of challenges to the U.S. mental health and social services delivery systems. Conditions that lead to the displacement of millions of refugees—wars, oppression, persecution, and poverty—are usually connected with economic and social factors related to underdevelopment. By improving social and economic conditions in the global South, the United States would decrease the need for people to leave their countries involuntarily.
- Because the illegal drug problem in the United States is connected to poverty in the global South, assistance with economic development can be viewed as preventive intervention in dealing with substance abuse. More than 26 million North Americans

abuse illegal drugs, and an estimated four-fifths of these narcotics—including almost all the heroin and cocaine—come from other countries (UN Development Programme, 1994). The primary illegal drug–producing countries are in the global South. For example, coca, which is used to make cocaine, is grown by poor Latin American and South American farmers who can make several times the profits selling coca that they could get from other crops. The United States has been blamed for creating an incentive for farmers to divert crops from coffee to coca because of its failure to support the renewal of an international coffee agreement that triggered a 50 percent drop in world coffee prices (Kerschner, 1991). Moreover, the income generated from drug-related crops helps the debt-ridden poor countries repay their foreign loans. Unless people in the global South have hope for other means of survival, they will continue to grow illegal drugs, and the United States will continue to have an enormous drug abuse problem.

WHAT YOU CAN DO

- Focus on the development needs identified by the communities in which you work. Take advantage of existing community structures and skills to combat poverty and exploitation.
- Learn about the outcome of the UN World Summit for Social Development, held in Copenhagen on March 6–12, 1995. Information on the UN Declaration for Social Development and the Program of Action is available from Lilian Chatterjee, ICSW Information, International Council on Social Welfare (380 Saint-Antoine Street West, Suite 3200, Montreal, Quebec, Canada H2Z 3X7; phone 514-287-3280, fax 514-987-1567).
- Learn about the Universal Declaration of Human Rights (UN, 1985). Adopted by the UN in 1948, the declaration was the first statement on the fundamental rights of all human beings. Its provisions have been incorporated into the laws and constitutions of many countries.

- Organize a teach-in on the politics of welfare reform at your college or university. One such event took place at the Graduate School of Social Service, Fordham University, New York City, in June 1994. Its goals: to protest recent welfare reform proposals that blame social problems on poor families, to dispel myths about the current debate on welfare reform, and to call for change.
- Learn about structural adjustment programs and their consequences. A good place to start is to read Danaher's (1994) *50 Years Is Enough.*

REFERENCES

Alliance for a Global Community. (1995). Hunger: Here and there. *Connections, 2*(2).

Boulding, E. (1995, February). The many dimensions of peacebuilding. *Hunger TeachNet, 6*(1), 8–11.

Breslin, P. (1995, April). On these sidewalks of New York, the sun is shining again. *Smithsonian, 26*, 100–111.

Danaher, K. (Ed.). (1994). *50 years is enough: The case against the World Bank and the International Monetary Fund.* Boston: South End Press.

Dasgupta, S. (1968). Gandhian concept of nonviolence and its relevance today to professional social work. *Indian Journal of Social Work, 29*, 113–122.

DiNitto, D. (1995). *Social welfare: Politics and public policy* (4th ed.). Boston: Allyn & Bacon.

Epstein, G., Graham, J., & Nemhard, J. (1993). *Creating a new world economy: Forces of change and plans for action.* Philadelphia: Temple University Press.

GATT and NAFTA: How trade agreements can change your life. (n.d.). (Available from Global Exchange, 2017 Mission Street, Room 303, San Francisco, CA 94110; phone 415-255-7296)

Hawkins, D. (1990). Explaining the black homicide rate. *Journal of Interpersonal Violence, 5*, 151–163.

Hunger 1995: Causes of hunger. (1995).(Available from Bread for the World Institute, 1100 Wayne Avenue, Suite 1000, Silver Spring, MD 20910; phone 301-608-2400)

Just 1%. (1995). (Brochure available from InterAction, 1717 Massachusetts Avenue, NW, Suite 801, Washington, DC 20036; phone 202-667-8227)

Kerschner, H. (1991). *A primer on international development.* Washington, DC: American Association for International Aging.

Lippmann, T. (1996, June 18). U.S. loses rank in global giving. *Washington Post.*

Lourie, N. V. (1968, September 28). *Poverty is violence.* Speech given at a meeting of the Women's Inter-national League for Peace and Freedom, Philadelphia.

Maathai, W. (1988). *The green belt movement.* Nairobi, Kenya: Environment Liaison Center International.

New York City NASW Center on Poverty, Violence, and Development. (1994). [Untitled report submitted to the Violence and Development Project]. New York: Author.

Ngaiza, A. (1989). Tanzania: A life-saving clinic in remote Chanika. In D. De Silva (Project Coordinator), *Against all odds: Breaking the poverty trap* (pp. 27–42). Washington, DC: Panos Institute.

Rohr, J. (1989). Introduction. In J. Rohr (Ed.), *The Third World: Opposing viewpoints* (pp. 12–15). San Diego: Greenhaven Press.

Schiller, B. R. (1989). *The economics of poverty and discrimination.* Englewood Cliffs, NJ: Prentice Hall.

Sherman, A. (1994). *Wasting America's future: The Children's Defense Fund report on the costs of child poverty.* Boston: Beacon Press.

Shuman, M. (1994). *Towards a global village: International community development initiatives.* Boulder, CO: Pluto Press.

UNICEF. (1994). *Progress of Nations 1994.* New York: UNICEF House.

United Nations. (1985). *The United Nations chronicle.* New York: Author.

United Nations. (1995a). *Families: The heart of society* (World Summit for Social Development issue paper). New York: United Nations Department of Public Information.

United Nations. (1995b). *NGOs: Partners in social development* (World Summit for Social Development issue paper). New York: United Nations Department of Public Information.

United Nations. (1995c). *Shelter, employment and the urban poor* (World Summit for Social Development issue paper). New York: United Nations Department of Public Information.

United Nations Development Programme. (1994). *Human development report, 1994.* New York: Oxford University Press.

United Nations Development Programme. (1995). *Human development report, 1995.* New York: Oxford University Press.

U.S. budget for FY '97. (1996). Washington, DC: Office of Management and Budget.

Wines, M., & Pear, R. (1996, July 30). President finds benefits in defeat of health care. *New York Times,* pp. A1, B8.

Yunus, M. (1994). Redefining development. In K. Danaher (Ed.), *50 Years is enough: The case against the World Bank and the International Monetary Fund* (pp. ix–xii). Boston: South End Press.

ADDITIONAL RESOURCES

InterAction: American Council for Voluntary International Action
1717 Massachusetts Avenue, NW, Suite 801
Washington, DC 20036
Phone: 202-667-8227
    An umbrella organization for several hundred international development agencies that address the issue of poverty around the world.

International Council on Social Welfare
380 Saint-Antoine Street West, Suite 3200
Montreal, Quebec, Canada H2Z 3X7
Phone: 514-287-3280; fax: 514-987-1567
    An organization that addresses international social welfare policies and issues and holds an international conference for social welfare professionals.

Oxfam America
26 West Street
Boston, MA 02111
Phone: 617-482-1211
    An international development agency that fights poverty and hunger. It produces educational materials, including videos, and conducts an annual educational campaign, the Fast for a World Harvest.

PART 3

VIOLENCE AGAINST WOMEN AND CHILDREN

BEYOND A FAMILY AFFAIR

Violence within the context of the family is a social problem with which the social work profession has been deeply concerned. However, violence against women and children does not occur in the isolation of the home. Rather, it is deeply embedded in a global ideology of male superiority that makes women and children particularly vulnerable to violence in all domains.

Violence against women worldwide is pervasive and serious, yet the problem was denied for a long time. According to the World-Watch Institute (Heise, 1989), "Violence against wives, indeed violence against [females] in general, is as old as recorded history, and cuts across all societies and socioeconomic groups. There are few phenomena so pervasive and yet so ignored" (p. 12).

The issue of violence within the family was first raised as a serious concern in 1975 at the International Women's Year World Conference in Mexico City (United Nations [UN], 1975a, 1975b). However, it was not until the 1980 Mid-Decade World Conference for Women in Copenhagen that the need to eliminate all forms of violence against women was fully recognized, and the Convention on the Elimination of All Forms of Discrimination Against Women was endorsed (UN, 1980).

Gender violence became a prominent issue at the 1985 World Conference on Women in Nairobi (UN, 1985). For the first time, women came together as activists for change within the international community. Violence against women is now considered "a serious issue and the subject of worldwide debate. The problem has been recognized as a serious obstacle to development and peace" (UN, 1989b, p. 3).

The rights of children also received international recognition with the passage of the Declaration on the Rights of the Child by the UN General Assembly in November 1989 (UN, 1989a). The declaration calls on nations to protect children from all forms of violence and exploitation.

Part 3 explores the pervasiveness of violence against women and children. It examines how violence obstructs the healthy development of individuals and societies and how the lack of development opportunities fuels violence and discusses what has been done and what still needs to be done to prevent violence against women.

GENDER VIOLENCE: A GLOBAL PROBLEM

Much of the violence that is directed toward women is rooted in economic, political, cultural, and religious systems that ensure male domination and control. Because violence against women is normalized to such a large extent, it is not considered unusual behavior when women are murdered, assaulted, sexually abused, threatened, or humiliated by their male partners (UN, 1989b). Traditions and social systems legitimate gender discrimination beginning at birth (Anderson & Moore, 1993).

Although the various dimensions of violence against women throughout the world have not been sufficiently documented, the following statistics shed light on its pervasiveness:

- In the United States, battery is the leading cause of injury to adult women (Koop, 1989).
- Domestic violence is estimated to occur in at least 70 percent of Mexican families (Carrillo, 1991).
- In Pakistan, at least one woman is burned alive by her husband each day, and there are many more cases that go unreported (Sennott, 1995).
- There are 100 million fewer females in Asia than would have been produced by normal birthrates owing to female infanticide, selective feeding of infants, and selective abortion practices (Clifton, 1995).
- The UN estimated that two out of three of the world's unschooled, and thus illiterate, people are female (Minnesota NASW chapter Center, 1994).

The widespread cultural belief that women are inferior gives rise to inequity, which in itself is a form of violence. In the global South, girls are more likely than are boys to be given less food, denied access to education and health care, forced into hard labor sooner, denied any kind of economic return on their labor, made to marry as young teenagers, bought and sold like slaves for prostitution and labor, and killed by sex-selective abortions and female infanticide (Minnesota NASW chapter Center, 1994).

Women also suffer from additional forms of violence that are officially sanctioned:

- Many of the world's political prisoners are women activists who have spoken out against gender-based violence.
- More women than men die as a result of armed conflicts.
- The majority of women do not enjoy basic human and civil rights in many countries. Although some countries have laws against gender inequity, these laws are often not enforced (Minnesota NASW chapter Center, 1994).
- Women still earn 30 percent to 40 percent less than do their male counterparts for comparable work (*Hunger 1995*, 1995).

VIOLENCE AGAINST CHILDREN

Like women, children are victims of many forms of violence, both inside and outside the home. According to Childhelp USA, one in three girls and one in eight boys are sexually abused in the United States before age 18 (Rohr, 1990). The majority of child sexual abuse in this country is perpetrated by someone known to the children—usually their fathers, stepfathers, or father substitutes. Although there is limited information about family sexual abuse in the global South, studies done in the Philippines, Sri Lanka, and Thailand suggest that the extent of the problem is similar to that of the United States (Centre for the Protection of Children's Rights, 1991; Doek, 1991).

Another form of child abuse that has gained notoriety in recent years is the selling of children for sex to tourists and other international visitors in Asian, African, and Latin American countries. Children are also involved in prostitution in disturbingly large numbers in Western Europe and North America, and there are reports of a growth in child sexual exploitation in the former Communist countries of Eastern Europe. The perpetrators are almost always male, whereas the children who are exploited are both male and female—although girls constitute by far the greatest proportion of the victims (Ireland, 1993).

The following quotation illustrates the magnitude of violence against children worldwide:

> The stories pour forth in an avalanche of horror. From Bosnia, young girls raped . . . and murdered. From Angola, Cambodia, Afghanistan, Mozambique, children literally torn to shreds by land-mines. . . . From Brazil, a paramilitary massacre of street children while they sleep in the quiet shadows of a church. From Thailand, young girls, stolen from their Myanmar villages, to be locked in brothels, servicing male sexual predators. From Somalia, Sudan, Rwanda, child refugees on the run . . . fleeing civil war, cut down in their flight by mortars, bullets, machetes. (UNICEF, 1994)

OBSTACLES TO DEVELOPMENT

Male Domination

A faith in violence as a solution to problems and militaristic values at the structural level results in boys being programmed to assume roles of dominance and male supremacy. There seems to be a connection between this culturally programmed desire for dominance and the fact that so many men around the world turn to violence against women (Pogrebin, 1990). The low economic position of women (and children) is linked with their vulnerability to violence, particularly in their households. The subordination of women in society allows them to be victims of violence. "Violence against women is a function of the belief, fostered in all cultures, that men are superior and that the women they live with are their possessions or chattels that they can treat as they wish and as they consider appropriate" (UN, 1989b, p. 33).

Militarism

> Left to sustain the family and endure the loneliness and vulnerability of separation, women suffer great hardships in wartime. Their houses may be damaged, or they may flee from home for fear of their lives. Dwindling food supplies and hungry children exacerbate tensions. And so, to the loss of husbands, fathers, sons and brothers who are killed in battle, is added the suffering of further deprivation. Often defenseless against invasion, women can find that armed conflict means rape and other forms of abuse by occupying troops, as well as a loss of the means of livelihood. (Vickers, 1993, p. 18)

Women are affected by war in a multitude of ways:
- In 1992, more people were killed in wars than at any time throughout the Cold War. Women and children were the primary victims of those wars (Sivard, 1993).
- Women are extremely vulnerable to rape, torture, and exploitation during military conflicts. There is growing international recognition that rape is being used as a tactic or prize of war (UN Development Programme, 1994).

- Of the people who are killed by antipersonnel mines, 30 percent to 40 percent are women and children (UN Development Programme, 1994).
- Of the world's refugees, 80 percent are women and their dependent children (*Hunger 1995*, 1995).
- As of 1994, approximately 200,000 children had been recruited to be soldiers. These children have been separated from their families, denied a normal life, subjected to military training that has distorted their values, and traumatized by war experiences (*Children at War*, 1994; InterAction, 1994).

In addition, unprecedented military spending in both the global North and the global South since the 1970s has slowed progress in the areas of health, education, and other basic needs in many parts of the world. This lack of progress has adversely affected the health and status of women and has made it difficult for poor women to get the services they need for themselves and their children (Sivard, 1993).

Domestic Violence

Domestic violence is a form of control that puts women's health—and lives—at risk, denies them their human rights, and hinders their full participation in society. For example, case studies of victims of domestic violence in Peru and Mexico revealed that men frequently beat their wives to demand the income these women had earned (Vasquez & Tamayo, 1989). A project of the Working Women's Forum in Madras, India, almost collapsed when the most articulate and energetic women started to drop out because of increasing domestic violence against them as a result of their involvement in the project (Carillo, 1992).

Domestic violence also affects children's development. A Canadian study reported high incidences of posttraumatic stress disorder, clinical dysfunction, and behavioral and emotional disorders in children from violent homes (Jaffe, Wilson, & Wolfe, 1986).

Unfortunately, the institutional response to family violence is often inadequate. Almost universally, the social impulse is to preserve the family at all costs, even if doing so compromises a woman's safety. As a high court judge in Uganda expressed, "It is better for one person to suffer rather than risk a complete breakdown of family life" (Heise, 1989, p. 13).

Changing Political and Economic Systems

Political and economic changes that affect poor people frequently lead to the disruption of traditional ways of life and hence cause social norms and established means of providing for the community to unravel. In addition to the breakdown in old systems, adequate alternatives are rarely in place to support people's needs. These desperate circumstances create conditions of "every man for himself." In the process, women and children often emerge as the most vulnerable (UN, 1989b; personal correspondence between Violence & Development Project and K. Kusterer, March 18, 1995).

One example of this problem is the worldwide trend toward the urbanization of rural peoples after their traditional ways of life have been disrupted by outside influences. Rapid urbanization and migration result in underemployment and underdevelopment, including the lack of access to basic resources and services. In such situations, a precarious economic existence is inevitable, and in people's struggle to survive, violence is often a result (Wetzel, 1993).

Absence of Development Opportunities

Underdevelopment, juxtaposed with a fiercely materialistic culture, feeds violence in the United States. It has been suggested that increasing violence is the result of "the sullen rage of mostly boys and young men who live in poverty and are taunted by visions of affluence and ease which they have no hope of reaching" (Washington Spectator, 1990, p. 171).

Inadequate development also seems to be a significant cause of violence in the lives of children in the global South. For example, nearly all Latin America's street children, 10 percent to 30 percent of whom are female, are engaged in some form of economic activity on the streets to support themselves or to supplement their families' incomes. Many report feeling proud to bring their earnings home to their families. Seventy-five percent of the girls on Latin America's streets are there to help meet their family's economic needs, with their parents' blessing (Rizzini & Lusk, 1995). However, living on the streets makes children vulnerable to prostitution, drug abuse, violence, and death. On average, six street children in Columbia and four in Brazil are killed each day (Castilho, 1995).

WHY RAISE THE STATUS OF WOMEN?

Basically, two arguments are made for raising the status of women; providing girls and women with more opportunities; and eliminating harmful customs against girls and women, such as the preference, of parents in some cultures, for having boys: the equity argument and the efficiency argument. The equity argument claims that it is unfair to women and girls when resources are distributed or withheld on the basis of sex, when women are not given equal educational and work opportunities, and when women's human rights are violated.

The efficiency argument claims that improving the status of girls and women will allow women to be part of the economic and social development of their countries and, therefore, will benefit everyone. This argument claims that it is inefficient and wasteful not to include women in development programs and points to studies that have found that women who have incomes spend their money to improve the lives of their children and communities more than do men. Thus, development progresses faster (Gross, 1993).

SUSTAINABLE HUMAN DEVELOPMENT: AN ANTIDOTE TO VIOLENCE AGAINST WOMEN AND CHILDREN

Many of the development issues that affect woman and children are the same in both the United States and the global South: violence in the home, community, and society at large; the absence of public money or the commitment to address social problems; low wages; and the lack of access to economic opportunities. To address these problems, two approaches have been suggested.

Gender-Sensitive Development

Development experts have come to realize that investing in women is the surest way to improve life for all because women have the primary responsibility for the well-being of the family and the community (*Hunger 1995*, 1995). Tisch and Wallace (1994) suggested that a gender analysis should be integrated into the conception, design, and implementation of all development projects. Such an analysis would take into account the impact of a project on women's and men's roles and responsibilities.

Development initiatives should involve women at every stage of planning and execution to ensure that their perspective and needs are fully accounted for (Tisch & Wallace, 1994). Far too often, projects are designed without consulting women, with the result that sometimes the amount of work they are required to do is increased. For example, when improved plowing techniques were introduced in Kenya, male farmers were able to double the number of acres they could plant. The project, however, also doubled the already taxing workload of women, because traditionally it was the women's job to weed the fields—by hand (*Hunger 1995*, 1995).

The following recommendations, proposed by the International Center for Research on Women (1993), are designed to promote gender-sensitive development:
- develop economic opportunities for women in private enterprise, in agriculture, and all sectors of formal employment
- close the gender gap in literacy and education
- increase women's reproductive choices by providing accessible, high-quality health and family planning services
- ensure that development efforts balance long-term environmental sustainability and women's subsistence and economic needs based on natural resources
- ensure that emergency and development assistance programs take into account women's roles, needs, and human rights in times of conflict, famine, disease, and rapidly changing economic and political circumstances.

Development That Addresses Violence against Women

As Heise (as quoted in Carillo, 1991) noted:

> The development community has come to realize that problems such as high fertility, deforestation and hunger cannot be solved without women's full participation. Yet, women cannot lend their labor or creative ideas fully when they are burdened with the physical and psychological scars of violence. (p. 11)

It is clear that attempts to integrate women into development are doomed to failure if they do not make violence against women the central issue (Women's Feature Service, 1993). Development agencies can make an important contribution by documenting the obstacles that gender violence places in the path of development and by identifying strategies for countering them. Carrillo (1992) argued that the development community should support projects that address gender violence as legitimate projects in themselves. Some efforts that have been made to counter violence against women include these:
- In Bombay, "ladies-only" cars were set aside in the mass transit system to prevent women from being harassed by men as they traveled to work (Carrillo, 1992).
- In Tempoal, Mexico, staff at the United Nations Development Fund for Women project worked with husbands and other members of the community to address the increased violence that emerged as a result of women's changing roles (Carrillo, 1992).
- In Cambodia, where efforts are under way to rebuild the nation after many years of war, a study was conducted to assess the legal rights of Cambodian women and the prevalence of domestic violence (study by the Asia Foundation, reported in an interview with Kathy Zimmerman on *All Things Considered*, 1995).

CASE STUDIES

The following case studies provide inspiring accounts of how women in Nicaragua and in two regions of India are not only finding ways to heal from trauma but are becoming empowered to take control of their lives.

CASE STUDY 1
Women Healing from Violence in Nicaragua

San Pablo del Norte (a fictitious name), a small town in the northern mountains of Nicaragua, may seem quiet enough now, but in the 1980s it was the object of several Contra attacks. Although many families had sons and siblings who were fighting on opposing sides of the civil war, no one ever talked much about the divisions that might have been caused. The Contra sympathizers went to military camps in Honduras, and the families they left behind kept silent about the ones who had clearly chosen another path.

After the war officially ended, the Contras euphorically returned home, many of them with their families. Their sense of euphoria was short-lived, however, as they restlessly and resentfully looked for land to farm (there was none) and a way to survive. Most of the tools and building materials promised by the government in exchange for weapons never arrived. Families who had been silent about their divisions during the war were now publicly splitting apart; whole communities became polarized.

Even the women, whose interest in politics was minimal (they primarily cared about food, clothing, and shelter for their loved ones), were affected by ruptures in the community. Each woman was identified by the side her husband had taken. There were angry quarrels, ugly rumors, and rampant distrust.

This was the situation that faced two women who came to San Juan del Norte as representatives of the Nicaraguan Network for the Promotion of Mental Health. Their intention was to help the women of the town to understand that they had human rights and that they could organize— beginning with mutual help and support groups— to find ways to improve their lives and those of their children.

This was no easy task. Even after the women agreed to meet, they stared at each other with anger, remembering the unspeakable harm done by the war, and refused to speak. Weeks and months later, the silence was broken, when little by little the women began to speak pieces of their truth more openly. The women continued to stare at each other, but now in amazement at their common stories. In time, the stories came pouring out like rivers in full flood: tales of hunger, death, and sickness and nothing to give the children; tales of unending grief for fallen loves ones and the land that once was their home; and tales of bitter— sometimes murderous—hatred between brothers. The women moved closer together, huddling against the cruelty and chaos of the outside world to comfort one another in what they now recognized as their common misery and pain.

Despite recurring waves of distrust and disagreement in their groups, the women found they could work together collectively for their common good. Realizing that they shared a common grief was the glue that bound them together. Thus, they found solace in one another. They learned to trust each other enough to work in small cooperatives to improve the economic status of their families.

One *campesina* (woman farmworker), with work-worn hands and lines of sorrow etched in her face, stated with certainty and quiet pride, "It is men who make war. We women are the ones who know how to reconcile, to make peace" (case study contributed by Constance Fabunmi, Minnesota NASW chapter Center on Violence, Development, and Family Structure; used with permission of the author).

CASE STUDY 2
Kerala, India: Linking Family Structure with Violence and Violence Prevention

Several Christian religious orders are working to meet the needs of people in cities and villages throughout the state of Kerala by, for example, setting up hospice programs; homes for the elderly; and educational, counseling, and advocacy programs. One order, the Carmellite sisters, has initiated a combined program of education and advocacy for women that has been highly successful and may well be viewed as feminism at its best.

The Carmellite nuns have approached the issue of equal status for women with a two-pronged plan: instituting special courses for women in the educational institutions run by their order and providing individual advocacy on behalf of women who have been abused, violated, or mistreated.

The first line of defense is to educate women about their self-worth and intrinsic value as human beings who have both human and legal rights. For many women, these awareness-raising classes are their first exposure to this philosophy. When women become empowered to value themselves, the first step toward the prevention of violence has been taken. Subsequently, these women are provided with information about specific legal rights.

The Carmellite nuns have also developed a program of individual advocacy to combat specific occurrences of abuse and other forms of violence whenever and wherever it occurs. For example, a member of the religious community will go with a woman who is facing a particular trauma and intercede on her behalf with her accuser—opponent—often a government official or employee in the public sector. This action frequently involves making court appearances and interceding with judges or going to police stations and taking a stand with male police officers. The result of this intervention is that government officials listen to the woman and give her a "fair" hearing, whereas previously her testimony or viewpoint would have probably been ignored. Such advocacy is not always approached from a defensive posture; frequently, the nuns take an offensive position and help a woman initiate a needed action (such as obtaining child support payments from a deserting husband). Many favorable outcomes have been obtained through this process.

It is incredible that a male-oriented, Hindu-dominated society would tolerate such aggressive action by the nuns. One reason for the success of the program is that Kerala has a strong tradition of respect for individual religious rights. Another reason is that religious people (nuns, priests, and other clergy and gurus) are held in high regard. The populace is virtually in awe of the nuns. The order's schools are the best in Kerala, and it is considered highly desirable to attend them. Furthermore, the nuns are respected because in addition to their religious affiliation, they have the worldliness to operate major educational institutions successfully. Thus, their actions and words are perceived as credible. The Carmellites look forward to the day when the family structure in India will reflect equal human rights for all family members, including women and girls, and they can focus their efforts on prevention, rather than intervention (case study contributed by Marilyn J. Kennedy, Minnesota NASW chapter Center on Violence, Development, and Family Structure; used with permission of the author).

CASE STUDY 3

Annapurna Mahila Mandal: A Triumph of Women's Strength

In India, thousands of men pour into Bombay from the surrounding countryside to work in the city's thriving textile mills. In the poor neighborhoods (known as the *busti*) where the workers live, enterprising women have developed small catering businesses to feed the men. Along with exhausting workloads, these women contend with chronic indebtedness; they are forced to buy grains and other provisions on credit—often at annual interest rates of over 100 percent (*Update India*, 1991).

To address some of these problems, 14 determined women founded a small organization in 1973 that they aptly named Annapurna Mahila Mandal, after the Hindu goddess of food. For almost 10 years, Annapurna operated entirely on volunteer labor and donated space and money. Then, in 1982, with help from international development agencies, it opened a multipurpose facility with paid staff to support its expanding program: loan services, a medical clinic, legal counseling, and vocational skills training.

Thousands of members of Annapurna have since borrowed millions of rupees from a revolving loan fund that boasts an almost perfect repayment record. By providing women caterers with capital support, equipment, and training, the organization has liberated its members from exploitative money lenders. Now that their catering businesses are more secure, women have become free to tackle new challenges: campaigning against dowries, domestic violence, and other discriminatory laws and practices.

Annapurna has been so successful that it has expanded its operations to Vashi, on the outskirts of Bombay. In addition to catering food for nearby factories and offices, the Vashi center provides a temporary home to women who are destitute, abused, or abandoned by their husbands.

One of Annapurna's most important contributions is instilling a sense of dignity in women. Prema Purao, one of the founders of Annapurna, tells the women: "Your work is important and worthy of pride" (*Update India*, 1991, p. 4). By changing the way women think about themselves, Annapurna is improving the lives of extended families and entire communities.

WHAT YOU CAN DO

- Learn what women's groups are doing in countries of the global South to stop violence and promote development.
- Advocate to increase the number of women in leadership positions in the United Nations, international development organizations, and U.S. development projects.
- Read about the outcomes of the Fourth UN World Conference on Women, held in Beijing, China, in September 1995 (see, for example, UN, 1995).
- Advocate for the increased availability of child care services and health insurance for workers and for laws and regulations that prohibit gender discrimination.
- Remember that early attitudes about gender roles and gender violence are shaped in school. Therefore, ensure that children are taught that violence against women is unacceptable and that sexual harassment and abuse in the schools will not be tolerated.

REFERENCES

All things considered. (1995, August 31). Interview with Kathy Zimmerman. [Study funded by Asia Foundation, 465 California Street, San Francisco, CA 94105; phone 415-982-4640]. Washington, DC: National Public Radio.

Anderson, J., & Moore, M. (1993, February 14–18). Born oppressed: Women in the developing world face cradle to grave discrimination, poverty. *Washington Post*, pp. 1–6.

Carrillo, R. (1991). Violence against women: An obstacle to development. In Center for Women's Global Leadership, *Gender violence: A development and human rights issue* (pp. 19–41). Highland Park, NJ: Plowshares Press.

Carrillo, R. (1992). *Battered dreams: Violence against women as an obstacle to development.* New York: United Nations Development Fund for Women.

Castilho, C. (1995, January). Children to the slaughter: Street life is deadly in Latin American countries. *World Paper*, p. 12.

Centre for Protection of Children's Rights. (1991). *Report on child rights violations: Annual report to 31 December 1991.* Bangkok, Thailand: Author.

Children at war. (1994). (Available from Save the Children, 52 Wilton Road, Westport, CT 06880; phone 203-221-4000)

Clifton, T. (1995, August 25). Asia's disappearing girls. *Minneapolis Star Tribune*, p. 16A.

Doek, J. E. (1991). Management of child abuse and neglect at the international level: Trends and perspectives. *Child Abuse and Neglect, 15*(1), 51–56.

Gross, S. H. (1993). *How-to-do-it manual: Ideas for teaching about contemporary women in Africa, Asia, and Latin America.* St. Louis Park, MN: Upper Midwest Women's History Center.

Heise, L. (1989, March–April). Crimes of gender. *World Watch*, pp. 12–21.

Hunger 1995: Causes of hunger. (1995). (Available from Bread for the World Institute, 1100 Wayne Avenue South, Suite 1000, Silver Spring, MD 20910; phone 301-608-2400)

InterAction. (1994, July 18). Strategies for families in war zones in Africa. *Monday Developments, 12,* 13. (Available from InterAction, 1717 Massachusetts Avenue, NW, Suite 801, Washington, DC 20036; phone 202-667-8227)

International Center for Research on Women. (1993, February 19). *Women's issues in development cooperation: A call for action.* (Available from the Center at 1717 Massachusetts Avenue, NW, Suite 302, Washington, DC 20036; phone 202-797-0007)

Ireland, K. (1993, September). *Wish you weren't here: The sexual exploitation of children and the connection with tourism and international travel* (Working Paper No. 7). (Available from the Overseas Department, Save the Children, 52 Wilton Road, Westport, CT 06880; phone 203-221-4000)

Jaffe, P., Wilson, S., & Wolfe, D. A. (1986). Promoting changes in attitudes and understanding of conflict resolution among child witnesses of family violence. *Canadian Journal of Behavioral Science, 18,* 356.

Koop, C. E. (1989). *Violence against women: A global problem.* Presentation by the Surgeon General of the United States to the U.S. Public Health Service. Washington, DC: U.S. Government Printing Office.

Minnesota NASW chapter Center on Violence, Development, and Family Structure. (1994). *Analysis of the linkages between violence and development/underdevelopment within the context of family structure* (Report submitted to the Violence and Development Project). St. Paul, MN: Author.

Pogrebin, L. C. (1990). Restrictive gender roles create teen rapists. In J. Rohr (Ed.), *Violence in America: Opposing viewpoints* (pp. 187–190). San Diego: Greenhaven Press.

Rizzini, I., & Lusk, M. (1995). Children in the streets: Latin America's lost generation. *Children and Youth Services Review, 17(3),* 387–395.

Rohr, J. (Ed.). (1990). Introduction. In J. Rohr (Ed.), *Violence in America: Opposing viewpoints* (pp. 12–15). San Diego: Greenhaven Press.

Sennott, C. (1995, May 18). Rights groups battle burning of women in Pakistan. *Boston Globe,* p. 1.

Sivard, R. L. (1993). *World military and social expenditures 1993.* Washington, DC: World Priorities.

Tisch, S. J., & Wallace, M. B. (1994). *Dilemmas of development assistance: The what, why, and who of foreign aid.* Boulder, CO: Westview Press.

UNICEF. (1994). *Progress of nations 1994.* New York: UNICEF House, p. 37.

United Nations. (1975a). *Declaration of Mexico City: Report of the international women's year world conference, Mexico City, Mexico.* New York: Author.

United Nations. (1975b). *World plan of action: Report of the international women's year world conference, Mexico City, Mexico.* New York: Author.

United Nations. (1980). *Convention on the elimination of all forms of discrimination against women: Report of the mid-decade world conference for women, Copenhagen, Denmark.* New York: Author.

United Nations. (1985). *Nairobi forward-looking strategies for the advancement of women: Report of the end of decade world conference on women.* New York: Author.

United Nations. (1989a). *Declaration on the rights of the child.* New York: Author.

United Nations. (1989b). *Violence against women in the family.* New York: Author.

United Nations. (1995). *Platform for action: Report of the Fourth World Conference on Women, Beijing, China.* New York: Author.

United Nations Development Programme. (1994). *Human development report, 1994.* New York: Oxford University Press.

Update: India. (1991). (Available from Oxfam America, 26 West Street, Boston, MA 02111)

Vasquez, S. R., & Tamayo, L. G. (1989, May). *Violencia y legalidad.* Lima, Peru: CONCYTEC.

Vickers, J. (1993). *Women and war.* Atlantic Highlands, NJ: Zed Books.

Washington Spectator. (1990). Poverty promotes teen violence. In J. Rohr (Ed.)., *Violence in America: Opposing viewpoints* (pp. 170–175). San Diego: Greenhaven Press.

Wetzel, J. W. (1993). *The world of women: In pursuit of human rights*. New York: New York University Press.

Women's Feature Service. (1993). *The power to change: Women in the Third World redefine their environment*. Atlantic Highlands, NJ: Zed Books.

ADDITIONAL RESOURCES

Association for Women in Development
1511 K Street, NW, Suite 825
Washington, DC 20005
Phone: 202-628-0440
  An organization that works to define development based on women's perspectives and promotes research, policy, and practice to engage women fully in building a just and sustainable development process.

Center for Women's Global Leadership
Douglass College, Rutgers University
27 Clifton Avenue
New Brunswick, NJ 08903-0270
Phone: 908-932-8782
  A center that works to shape and advance women's rights and is helping to build the women's international human rights network.

Women's Commission for Refugee Women
  and Children
International Rescue Committee
122 East 42nd Street
New York, NY 10016-1289
Phone: 212-551-3086
  An advocacy and expert-resource organization that deals with issues facing uprooted women and children. It sends delegations to refugee settings that observe and make recommendations for improving conditions and provides an educational program for high school teachers and students about the experience of refugees.

PART 4

The world is enriched by the ethnic and cultural diversity of the people who inhabit it. Yet few countries are untouched by ethnic and racial violence. Despite the United States' claim to being a true melting-pot society, the mass media are filled with accounts of intergroup conflict, hate crimes, and random acts of violence perpetrated on the basis of people's skin color, ethnicity, and religious affiliation. Meanwhile, ethnic conflict is rife in many other parts of the world, including the Middle East, Central Asia, Africa, and post-Communist Eastern Europe, sending a steady stream of immigrants to the United States and other relatively stable countries.

Ethnic violence is of particular concern to the social work profession, which has a long history of working to promote social justice for oppressed populations. By working with people from different ethnic groups, professionals in the field have developed an understanding of the complex relationships between poverty and prejudice and each group's role in interethnic conflict based on their history of domination or subordination.

Part 4 explores some of the various causes and consequences of racial and ethnic conflict around the world. It examines the link between ethnic violence in the United States and the global South and discusses how the lack of development opportunities fuels ethnic violence and how sustainable human development can help alleviate this global problem.

ETHNICITY AND ETHNOVIOLENCE DEFINED

Ethnic Groups and Ethnicity

Ethnic groups are made up of people united by any combination of the following: culture, religion, language, dialect, geographic origin, traditions, values, and symbols (Thernstrom, Orlov, & Handlin, 1980). Estimates of the number of distinct ethnic groups in the world range from 575 groups that are either current national states or have the potential to claim that status to 5,000 different ethnic groups based on distinct languages (Nielsson & Jones, 1993, cited in Gurr, 1993; Nietschmann, 1987). Pinderhughes (1989) defined ethnicity as

> connectedness based on commonalities where specific aspects of cultural patterns are shared and where transmission over time creates a common history. . . . Race, while a biological term, takes on ethnic meaning when and if members of that biological group have evolved specific ways of living. . . . Ethnic values and practices foster the survival of the group and of individuals within. (p. 6)

Ethnoviolence

Ethnoviolence refers to violence perpetrated primarily on the basis of one's ethnicity. There is no single cause of ethnic violence. Rather, it stems from multiple, interrelated factors, including the following:

- hateful revenge and territorial disputes, often based on a history of dominant and subordinate relationships between two groups
- injustice and the unequal distribution of economic resources and political power
- repression and neglect of minority populations
- competition over limited resources
- prejudice and ignorance (*Conflict and Development*, 1994; Pacific Northwest NASW Center, 1994).

TYPES OF HATE CRIMES

Thrill Hate Crimes

In thrill hate crimes, offenders target violence against individuals from another group—often Asians, Hispanics, gay men and lesbians, or African Americans—to give themselves a thrill. The victims are often interchangeable. Some offenders substitute one victim for another when their first choice for attack is unavailable, and one member of a disfavored group can easily replace another. Because of the growing "culture of hate," for many people hate has become hip and intolerance is "in." Random attacks of hate reflect the increasing social acceptability of violence and group stereotyping ("Landmark Study Reveals," 1995).

Defensive Hate Crimes

Defensive hate crimes occur in response to incidents that the perpetrators perceive as intrusion by outsiders. These perpetrators have a stronger commitment to prejudice than their counterparts who commit thrill hate crimes. Defensive hate crimes generally involve a series of attacks perpetrated by white men, often acting alone. The perpetrators are trying to send a specific message that their victims do not belong in a particular community, school, or workplace and that anyone in the victim's group who dares "intrude" could be next ("Landmark Study Reveals," 1995).

Mission Hate Crimes

Mission hate crimes are the most serious but rarest of all hate crimes. The perpetrator has fully committed himself to prejudice and has allowed bigotry to take over his life. Frequently, he has joined a local chapter of the Ku Klux Klan or a neo-Nazi or Skinhead group to be closer to those who espouse similar beliefs. This type of perpetrator usually has failed to fit into society and blames his personal failures on the members of any group he believes to be different. His mission is more than to target a particular victim; he is seeking to rid the world of all members of the "inferior" group, as well as its symbols ("Landmark Study Reveals," 1995).

CASE STUDIES

Roxbury: A Thrill Hate Crime

One winter evening, three 22-year-old white men, bored and looking for something to do, decided to go out and "start some trouble." They picked up several bricks from a construction site and drove to Roxbury, a predominately black section of Boston. As they were driving, they saw a 42-year-old African American man walking alone near his home. The three young men drove up behind the victim and struck him with one of the bricks. Then they quickly drove out of the area and back to their homes ("Landmark Study Reveals," 1995).

San Francisco: A Defensive Hate Crime

A 32-year-old Asian American male cabdriver was driving through a neighborhood in San Francisco. When the taxi stopped at a traffic light, a 19-year-old local white man smashed a hockey stick through the cab's rear window. He warned the cabdriver to leave the area and told him that he did not belong in the United States ("Landmark Study Reveals," 1995).

Medway: A Mission Hate Crime

Four white male Skinheads from Medway, a suburb of Boston, had previously painted swastikas on public structures in and around their town, but had not been arrested for any of these incidents. The four youths began to escalate their violence until they drove to the South End of Boston one night, looking for gays to bash. They approached two white men they thought were gay and began to harass them verbally. When the victims attempted to escape, the Skinheads took baseball bats from their van and beat the men. Upon arresting the four perpetrators, two of whom had White Power tatoos on their bodies, the Boston police discovered that their van and their homes were full of hate literature ("Landmark Study Reveals," 1995).

ETHNOVIOLENCE: A GLOBAL PROBLEM

Throughout the world, ethnic conflict is rooted in relationships in which one group dominates another based on an ideology of superiority. The "superior" group seeks to preserve its power and privileges through violence or the threat of violence against those it perceives as different or inferior (McLemore, 1994). Ethnoviolence on the personal level, combined with collusion at the institutional level, functions as a kind of terrorism (Sheffield, 1995). In his autobiographical novel *Black Boy*, Wright (1937) noted: "The things that influenced my conduct as a Negro did not have to happen to me directly: I needed but to hear of them to feel their full effects in the deepest layers of my consciousness. Indeed the white brutality that I had not seen was a more effective control of my behavior than that which I knew" (p. 65).

History of Violence

In the United States, white people became the dominant group through exploitation and force, beginning with violence committed against indigenous people by white European settlers in the 1600s. For decades, the government and its agents often institutionally organized and sanctioned hate violence. State violence was committed not only against Native Americans but also captured and enslaved Africans, free African Americans, and other racial groups (Weiss, 1990).

Violence based on hate has been both spontaneous and organized in the United States. Established hate groups have played an integral role in perpetuating an environment of fear for Americans from diverse racial and ethnic groups (Sheffield, 1995). The Ku Klux Klan, one of the better-known organized hate groups, has been responsible for some of the most brutal violence in American history. Between 1889 and 1941, the Klan lynched 3,811 African Americans in this country (Sheffield, 1995).

In recent years, hate crimes have been on the rise in the United States. Klan members have developed ties with a number of other hate groups, such as Holocaust denial groups, the neo-Nazi Skinhead movement, and the Aryan Nation. The movement as a whole has become more sophisticated in its organizing techniques. A survey of state and municipal law enforcement agencies reported a 19.3 percent rise in bias crimes during 1992 (*White Supremacy in the 90s*, 1994). In the early to mid-1990s, only 25,000 Americans were hard-core activists for the white supremacist movement, but approximately 200,000 people subscribed to racist publications, attended marches and rallies, and donated money to the cause. In addition, as of 1994, 150 independent racist radio and TV shows aired weekly, reaching millions of sympathizers (*White Supremacy in the 90s*, 1994).

Like the United States, the global South has a history of hate violence. In many countries, colonizing powers played a key role in igniting ethnic tensions that still exist. In Africa, for example, from the mid-15th to the mid-20th century, colonizing powers redrew national boundaries, usually ignoring well-established tribal cultural patterns. People were counted and classified in discrete and bounded groups; thus, new categories of identity were created to replace the overlapping and multiple cultural identities that had existed before. Furthermore, colonial state policies promoted differential treatment of ethnic groups, which led to extensive economic and social disparities. After independence, systems of inequity continued, fueling ethnic conflicts (Jalali & Lipset, 1993).

The violence goes on. Around the globe, ethnoviolence has reached alarming proportions. Most civil wars in the post–Cold War world have been ethnic, tribal, or religious in nature. From Serbs practicing "ethnic cleansing" of Muslims to Indonesian troops firing on unarmed protesters in

East Timor to police brutality in Los Angeles, hate violence is a global problem (Shuman & Harvey, 1993). As of 1992, 29 wars between ethnic groups raged worldwide. From these conflicts, 3,351,000 people, mostly civilians, died (Sivard, 1993).

ETHNOVIOLENCE AND DEVELOPMENT: MAKING THE CONNECTION

Militarism fuels ethnoviolence and impedes development. Although the causes of ethnic conflict are usually domestic or regional disputes, these disputes often escalate into armed confrontation when wealthier nations provide weapons or the financial means to purchase them (Deng & Zartman, 1991, cited in *Conflict and Development,* 1994). During the Cold War, both the United States and the Soviet Union provided military assistance to opposite sides in conflicts in the global South. These superpowers had a hand in driving violent ethnic conflicts in Sudan, Somalia, Angola, and Guatemala, for example. In the 1990s, the United States continues to be one of the top producers of weapons, and nations of the global South are major purchasers (Hartung, 1994).

In some countries, governments and armed forces have inflamed historic ethnic and religious tensions to consolidate their power and elite status. In Rwanda, for example, tensions between the Hutu and Tutsi ethnic groups have been systematically heightened by different rulers throughout history. German and Belgian colonial powers favored the Tutsis for their lighter skin and greater height. At independence in 1962, violence took the lives of 100,000 to 200,000 people. The ensuing years saw an ongoing struggle for control between the Tutsis and the Hutus. When a plane crash killed the Hutu presidents of Rwanda and Burundi in April 1994, the accident touched off a wave of ethnically based killings that left 500,000 dead. Subsequently, more than 1 million people fled to Zaire in one week in July 1994. Decades of development achievements have been destroyed (*Conflict and Development,* 1994; *Hunger 1995,* 1995).

Ethnoviolence obstructs development. Ethnic conflict generates multiple costs to society.

Among them are the
- denial of fundamental human rights and freedoms
- breakdown of political order
- displacement of thousands of people, mainly women and children, who are forced to flee their homes
- depletion of environmental resources, reducing the land's ability to produce crops and sustain people
- destruction of roads, bridges, food supplies, and other basic aspects of the infrastructure
- interruption of economic development and individuals' efforts to provide for themselves and their families (*Conflict and Development,* 1994).

Sudan is one country where interethnic war has had a devastating effect on human and societal development. In 1984, after years of state-sanctioned religious and economic oppression, the people in the southern half of Sudan (composed mostly of Christians and tribal groups) launched a guerrilla war against the Muslim-dominated northern half of the country, the home of the national government. Largely a subsistence-agriculture society in which people survive on the food they grow, Sudan was thrown into famine when war broke out and people were unable to plant or harvest their crops. More than 500,000 people had died in the conflict by 1994. Advances in development, such as schools, health clinics, and agricultural research programs, were destroyed throughout the country (*Conflict and Development,* 1994; *Hunger 1995,* 1995).

The lack of development opportunities leads to ethnoviolence. The UN Development Programme (1994) cited the lack of income security as one of the main root causes of ethnic violence in many countries. The fact that only one-quarter of the world's people are assured a basic, steady income helps explain why the planet is rife with competitive, ethnic conflict.

Social and economic inequity often correlate with racial and ethnic origin, constituting what can be called passive ethnoviolence (Dasgupta, 1968). Consider these statistics:
- In the United States, the unemployment rate for African Americans is twice that of white people (DiNitto, 1995).

- Poverty rates among African Americans and Hispanic Americans are nearly three times those of white people (UN Development Programme, 1994; Weiss, 1990).
- During South Africa's apartheid regime, if white South Africa had been a separate country, it would have ranked 24th in the world in human development, and black South Africa would have placed 123rd (*Hunger 1995*, 1995).
- In Guatemala, where Mayan Indians make up the majority of the population, the life expectancy for Mayan men is 48 compared to 65 for non-Mayan men (*Hunger 1995*, 1995).

Unjust development can lead to ethnoviolence. "Progress" itself can be a source of conflict when it serves the interests of wealthier people and excludes traditionally marginalized groups. For example, indigenous people around the world have had their traditional lands and resources usurped and exploited by vast logging, mining, and petroleum operations in the name of economic development. Their calls for justice have often been violently suppressed. In Nigeria, for instance, the extraction of petroleum from the lands of the Ogoni people has made the country among the richest in Africa, while the Ogoni continue to suffer from extreme poverty (*Conflict and Development*, 1994).

Unjust development takes other forms as well. Hoff and Polack (1993) pointed out that to meet international demands for the repayment of debts, governments of countries in the global South often force peasants to abandon their traditional, often environmentally sound, farming practices or to abandon their land altogether to produce cash crops for export. The results: the disruption of traditional ways of life, the destruction of local ecosystems, hunger, deprivation, indignity—all of which are forms of violence. Such conditions ultimately give rise to political instability and physical violence.

SUSTAINABLE HUMAN DEVELOPMENT: AN ANTIDOTE TO ETHNOVIOLENCE

As Rigoberto Menchú, of Guatemala, who received the Nobel Prize for Peace in 1992, stated:

It is not that peace is merely the absence of war, combat or conflict; rather, it is the absence of the conditions that give rise to war: intolerance, disrespect, arrogance, rigidity—and most of all, indignity and hunger. When people's needs and desires are satisfied, we can begin to talk about building peace. (Quoted in Oxfam America, 1992)

The basic premise of part 4 is that real solutions to ethnic violence lie in promoting sustainable human development. For the world to be a place where all people can live in safety, dignity, peace, and economic security, the following actions are needed:

- Encourage the redistribution of land, resources, and income to reduce the gap between the wealthy elite and the vast impoverished underclass.
- Promote strong, participatory democracies, in which people are given ample opportunities to be involved in decisions that affect their lives.
- Promote vibrant civil societies.
- Provide constitutional protections for racial and ethnic groups, which make a pluralistic society possible. The U.S. Supreme Court's enforcement of the Fourteenth Amendment to the Constitution ensures legal protection for American racial and ethnic groups. As a result, most civil rights movements in the United States have fought for pluralism and fairness, rather than for secession and separatism.
- Help nations become self-sufficient in the provision of such basic needs as food, safe water, shelter, clothing, and health care.
- Foster greater understanding among racial and ethnic groups and promote the peaceful resolution of conflicts (Shuman & Harvey, 1993).

Strong democratic systems and sustainable human development can go a long way toward eliminating sources of conflict. Nonetheless, some groups and nations will inevitably have disagreements with other groups and nations. When conflicts do occur, every attempt should be made to resolve them through nonviolent means.

Ethnic tensions can be reduced through programs that foster a greater understanding of the different cultures and life experiences of various ethnic groups. When possible, ethnic groups should be encouraged to discuss their historic differences and to forgive each other for past mistakes.

CIVIL SOCIETY: GIVING POWER TO THE PEOPLE

Civil society is the web of nongovernmental organizations and movements that empower citizens to take action and solve problems on their own behalf. Such organizations serve as a critical mechanism for creating new solutions to social, economic, and political problems at the grassroots level and for defusing potentially explosive situations that are fueled by governmental inaction.

In the United States, groups, such as the United Way, the National Association for the Advancement of Colored People, and labor unions, have played a key role in fighting racial injustice and seeking fair treatment and better working conditions for all citizens.

The videotape *Not in Our Town* (1995) tells the inspiring story of how Billings, Montana, took action against a wave of violent hate crimes that swept the community. The local painters union repainted the home of a Native American woman after it was spray painted with racist graffiti. The human rights coalition organized more than 100 community members to collect more than 6,000 signatures of support. After someone threw a cinderblock through the window of a Jewish child's bedroom because a menorah was displayed in the window, the local newspaper published a colorful full-page photograph of a menorah and asked people throughout Billings to put it in their window as an act of solidarity. More than 10,000 photographs were displayed. The rash of hate crimes stopped.

Elsewhere in the world, nongovernmental organizations are breaking new ground in fostering ethnic harmony. For example, the Neve Shalom Kibbutz, located between Jerusalem and Tel Aviv, has established the only Jewish–Arab bilingual school system in the country to promote the ideals of peaceful coexistence and equality between the two groups (American Friends of Neve Shalom, 1996).

WHAT YOU CAN DO

- Find out how you can become involved in the UN's International Decade of the World's Indigenous People, launched in December 1994. Contact Julian Burger, Centre for Human Rights (Palais des Nations, CH-1211 Geneva 10, Switzerland; phone 41-22-917-3413, fax 41-22-917-0212).
- Help prevent an anti-immigration backlash by initiating community-based educational activities, such as cultural awareness days.
- Get involved in grassroots organizing, intervention, and advocacy in ethnic communities.
- Advocate for strong democracies that include and involve all ethnic groups, both at home and overseas.
- Promote peace and social justice in all practice settings through the use of nonviolent conflict-resolution strategies.
- Work to reduce violence and ethnic stereotyping in the mass media.

REFERENCES

American Friends of Neve Shalom/Wahat Al-Salam. (1996). (Brochure available from the organization at 121 Sixth Avenue, Suite 502, New York, NY 10013; phone 212-226-9246)

Conflict and development. (1994). Washington, DC: Panos Institute.

Dasgupta, S. (1968). Gandhian concept of nonviolence and its relevance today to professional social work. *Indian Journal of Social Work, 29,* 113–122.

DiNitto, D. (1995). *Social welfare politics and public policy* (4th ed.). Boston: Allyn & Bacon.

Gurr, T. R. (1993). *Minorities at risk: A global view of ethnopolitical conflicts.* Washington, DC: U.S. Institute of Peace.

Hartung, W. D. (1994). *And weapons for all.* New York: HarperCollins.

Hoff, M. D., & Polack, R. J. (1993). Social dimensions of the environmental crisis: Challenges for social work. *Social Work, 38,* 204–211.

Hunger 1995: Causes of hunger. (1995). (Available from Bread for the World Institute, 1100 Wayne Avenue South, Suite 1000, Silver Spring, MD 20910; phone 301-608-2400)

Jalali, R., & Lipset, S. M. (1993). Racial and ethnic conflicts: A global perspective. In D. Caraley (Ed.), *New world politics: Power, ethnicity, and democracy* (pp. 55–76). Montpelier, VT: Capital City Press.

Landmark study reveals hate crimes vary significantly by offender motivation. (1995, August). *Klanwatch Intelligence Report* (Montgomery, AL), pp. 7–9.

McLemore, S. D. (1994). *Racial and ethnic relations in America.* Boston: Allyn & Bacon.

Nietschmann, B. (1987). The third world war. *Cultural Survival Quarterly, 11*(3), 1–6.

Not in Our Town [videotape]. (1995). (Available from We Do the Work, 5867 Ocean View Drive, Oakland, CA 94618; phone 510-547-8484)

Oxfam America. (1992). [Campaign materials for the Fast for a World Harvest]. (available from Oxfam America, 26 West Street, Boston, MA 02111; phone 617-482-1211)

Pacific Northwest NASW Center on Violence, Development, and Ethnicity (Idaho, Oregon, and Washington NASW chapters). (1994). *Research brief* (Summary report submitted to the Violence and Development Project). Portland, OR: Author.

Pinderhughes, E. (1989). *Understanding race, ethnicity and power.* New York: Free Press.

Sheffield, C. (1995). Hate-violence. In P. S. Rothenberg (Ed.), *Race, class and gender in the United States: An integrated study* (pp. 432–441). New York: St. Martin's Press.

Shuman, M., & Harvey, H. (1993). *Security without war: A post–Cold War foreign policy.* Boulder, CO: Westview Press.

Sivard, R. L. (1993). *World military and social expenditures 1993.* Washington, DC: World Priorities.

Thernstrom, S., Orlov, A., & Handlin, O. (Eds.). (1980). *Harvard encyclopedia of American ethnic groups.* Cambridge, MA: Belknap Press.

United Nations Development Programme. (1994). *Human development report, 1994.* New York: Oxford University Press.

Weiss, J. C. (1990). Violence motivated by bigotry: Ethnoviolence. In L. Ginsberg et al. (Eds.), *Encyclopedia of social work, 18th edition, 1990 supplement* (pp. 307–319). Silver Spring, MD: NASW Press.

White supremacy in the 90s. (1994). (Available from the Center for Democratic Renewal, PO Box 50469, Atlanta, GA 30302; phone 404-221-0025)

Wright, R. (1937). *Black boy.* New York: Harper & Bros.

ADDITIONAL RESOURCES

Center for Democratic Renewal
PO Box 50469
Atlanta, GA 30302-0469
Phone: 404-221-0025
   A national clearinghouse for information about the white supremacist movement in the United States.

Center on Rights Development
Graduate School of International Studies
University of Denver
Denver, CO 80208
Phone: 303-871-2523 or 303-871-2313
   An international human rights program that focuses on Africa and indigenous peoples' movements.

Panos Institute
1025 T. Jefferson St., Suite 105
Washington, DC 20007
Phone: 202-965-5177
   A research institute that publishes educational materials about the development process, including social conflict.

U.S. Committee for Refugees
1717 Massachusetts Avenue, NW, Suite 701
Washington, DC 20036
Phone: 202-347-3507
   An organization that documents conditions of refugees, asylum seekers, and persons who have been displaced by violence or persecution. Presses for humane treatment and the protection of human rights.

PART 5

ENDING THE GLOBAL EPIDEMIC

The production, distribution, and consumption of illegal drugs has become one of the world's most corrosive threats, spawning crime and violence around the globe (UN, Development Programme, 1994). The problem has reached such proportions that the international retail value of illicit drugs now exceeds that of the world's oil trade and is second only to worldwide arms sales (King & Schneider, 1991).

The widespread international commerce in narcotics has flooded the United States with drugs that endanger individuals, families, and entire communities. Most of the contraband entering the country has been grown by poor farmers in the global South and processed and distributed by drug lords who wield enormous political and economic power (Shuman & Harvey, 1993).

Part 5 focuses primarily on cocaine and its derivative, crack. More than any other popular drug in U.S. history, crack cocaine has caused social damage on an unprecedented scale. It induces violent behavior in users and is linked with the unparalleled rise in crime and murder rates in the United States since its appearance on the streets in the 1980s (DuPont, 1991).

The world's cocaine-producing countries are Peru; Bolivia; Colombia; and, to a lesser extent, Ecuador and Brazil (*Narcotics and Development*, 1993). The main cocaine-consuming nation is the United States, which uses 75 percent of the world's cocaine (Office of National Drug Control Policy, 1995). Both the drug-producing and drug-consuming countries are linked in a cycle of substance abuse and violence. Because the drug problem is global, it cannot be solved by any one nation alone; rather, it requires a comprehensive and coordinated international response. The real solution to the drug crisis lies in eradicating one of its main root causes—poverty and the lack of viable economic opportunities—by promoting sustainable human development.

THE POWER OF CRACK COCAINE

Cocaine is a narcotic substance derived from the coca plant, a bushy shrub that is native to South America. The coca plant has been sacred to the Indian populations of the Andes since pre-Incan times because of its medicinal qualities. Cocaine is only one of 14 alkaloids contained in the coca leaf, which contains more than 28 nutrients that supplement the daily diets of many Andean people (*Narcotics and Development*, 1993).

The hallmark of crack cocaine is its ability to induce persistent, intensive drug-seeking behaviors. Studies of animals have shown that the reinforcing properties of cocaine are enormous, producing a powerful craving that leads the user to abandon everything to satisfy a compulsion to obtain more of the drug (DuPont, 1991). The intensity and rapid onset of euphoria, combined with a strong craving that may develop, account for crack cocaine's strong potential for addiction. The use of crack cocaine is concentrated primarily in high-risk, urban communities throughout the United States, where its sale in inexpensive single doses has widened its accessibility. The drug's low cost; ease of administration; and fast, powerful effects have made it a formidable street drug (DuPont, 1991).

Hundreds of thousands of people have become addicted to cocaine, particularly crack. Addiction should be viewed as a disease—not as a failure of individual willpower—from which many individuals can recover. Appropriate education can prevent some people from becoming addicted. For those who do become "hooked," treatment, not punishment, is the solution (Schmoke, 1990).

DRUG–RELATED VIOLENCE: A GLOBAL AFFLICTION

This section discusses the three elements of the narcotics chain—production, trafficking, and consumption—and the effects of drugs, both in the United States and in the global South.

Production

Poor farmers in the global South often cultivate the coca plant for drug production as a means of survival. Although they receive only 1 percent of the ultimate street price of the drugs they grow, the average $1,000 a year they can earn producing coca is often 25 percent to 50 percent more than what they can earn from growing such crops as bananas, corn, and oranges (UN Development Programme, 1994). As a farmer from Bolivia said, "I have no fear of what I am doing. I am obligated to plant this coca to take care of my five children" (Sims, 1995, p. A3).

The cultivation of coca is appealing to farmers for other reasons as well. Unlike other crops, the coca plant requires little care and is harvested only three times a year. In contrast, traditional crops require years of hard labor before they yield any fruit and are much heavier to transport through the jungle (Sims, 1995).

Along with the difficulty of growing food crops and the low income earned from doing so, farmers in the global South face other challenges, including the absence of long-term government support and armed conflicts that disrupt traditional planting practices and irrigation systems. At the international level, South American countries face falling prices for typical exports, as well as an increasing international demand for illegal drugs (*Narcotics and Development*, 1993; Smith et al., 1992).

What happened in the Andes in the 1980s demonstrates how inadequate rural development contributes to the global drug crisis. After many mainstream agricultural initiatives to grow rubber, tobacco, coffee, and other crops failed, Colombian traffickers entered the Andes with coca seeds, demonstration plots, and venture capital, promising farmers that they would purchase their harvests. The Colombian cocaine "initiative" had a tremendous economic, social, and political impact on South America and the entire Western Hemisphere. Brazil experienced spiraling street crime as a result of cocaine consumption. Ecuador and Venezuela became centers for the laundering of drug money. Argentina saw an increase in drug traffickers, who exploited trade links with Europe. And Mexico and other countries became way stations en route to consumer markets, principally the United States (Smith et al., 1992).

Trafficking

Free trade and high-speed telecommunications have facilitated the smuggling of illicit narcotics out of the global South (Watson et al., 1993). Through an intricate network of drug-shipment routes and money-laundering bases, international drug-related crime organizations have managed to infiltrate countries around the world (Watson et al., 1993). Cooperation among such groups is increasing on an unprecedented scale (Atkinson, 1994). Moreover, these groups often have the help of legitimate organizations and individuals, including banks and other businesses and corrupt governmental officials (Andelman, 1994). During the summer of 1995, Colombia was rocked by allegations that its president, Ernesto Samper, had accepted nearly $6 million in campaign contributions from drug dealers in exchange for leniency in the courts. The Colombian defense minister resigned amid allegations that he had ordered a campaign treasurer to solicit money from major drug traffickers. "Political parties are losing credibility . . . the system itself is shaking," said

Francisco Thoumi, head of the Center for International Studies in Colombia (quoted in Schemo, 1995, p. 12).

The sale and use of narcotics in the global South has been accompanied by considerable violent crime. In Brazil, for example, gangs selling cocaine terrorize the *favelas* (slums) of Sao Paulo and Rio de Janeiro (Smith et al., 1992). In Colombia, 45 judges and 42 journalists were assassinated by drug thugs in the 1980s (Smith et al., 1992). In Mexico, drug traffickers are carving out an ever larger share of the world's drug trade. The bursts of violence that have attended the traffickers' rise have led many Mexicans to fear that their country is sliding toward the sort of terror the Medellin cocaine cartel unleashed on Colombia during the late 1980s and the early 1990s. From 1992 to 1995, victims have included the Roman Catholic cardinal of Guadalajara, two former state prosecutors, and more than a dozen active and retired federal police officers (Golden, 1995).

Narcotics trafficking has also had profound negative effects on entire economic systems by distorting local currencies, impeding foreign investments, depriving countries of tax revenues from traffickers, and discouraging legitimate development by offering higher wages than legal businesses (Smith et al., 1992).

As in the global South, narcotics trafficking has also created an alternative source of income in the United States. One of the most troubling results of the crack-cocaine craze has been the increase in violent gangs in American cities that are plagued by high unemployment, substandard educational systems, and the lack of services (Ostrowski, 1990). Forming an alternative economic system for people who otherwise feel shut out, the participation of gangs in the street cocaine trade creates an illegal source of revenue for people of all ages, even nine-year-old children who earn $100 a day serving as lookouts for dealers (Rohr, 1990). At the same time, the drug trade constrains legitimate economic development by fueling crime and violence.

When the sale and use of narcotics creates social turmoil, the institutional response of the police or military is often increased repressive violence (Van Soest & Bryant, 1995). For example, to wage the "War on Drugs," U.S. police SWAT teams and paramilitary task forces carry out sweeps in housing projects and mass evictions of drug suspects and their families. There have even been calls for deploying the National Guard and federal troops to patrol ghetto "war zones" (*Narcotics and Development*, 1993).

Consumption

As Representative Charles B. Rangel (D-NY) (quoted in Benjamin, 1990) eloquently stated:

> We have watched many of our young kids turn to dope to cope because they are without hope. America has watched and wept as many lives have become twisted and snuffed out by the powerful lure of drug addiction. (p. 82)

Drug consumption is at the other end of the narcotics chain. Most drug users and abusers live in the industrialized countries of the global North. In the United States, over 6 million users spent $31 billion on cocaine and crack in 1993 (Office of National Drug Control Policy, 1995). Their behavior often has enormous social, economic, and political consequences not only for them and their families but for society in general. On a monetary basis alone, drug-related crime, law enforcement, health care, and treatment cost the United States an estimated $29.1 billion a year (U.S. Department of Justice, 1994). Among violent offenders in state prisons, 50 percent reported being under the influence of alcohol or drugs at the time they committed the offenses, and 79 percent reported using drugs previously (U.S. Department of Justice, 1994).

Drug abuse is not limited to the global North, however. In recent years, some countries in the global South have experienced a dramatic increase in the consumption of hard drugs, particularly among young men in urban areas. The risk of drug addiction is particularly high in source countries, where cheap drugs are readily available. Many urban areas of the global South have several of the same troubling characteristics that thrive in parts of the United States: high unemployment, the lack of services, and inadequate or nonexistent educational opportunities (Smith et al., 1992).

A serious threat in the Andean region is the smoking of a mixture of coca paste and tobacco—called *pitillo* in Peru and Bolivia and *basuco* in Colombia—which can cause quick addiction and permanent brain damage because of the high concentration of chemical impurities in the drug. Colombia is estimated to have as many as 500,000 basuco smokers, mostly unemployed youths and other marginalized people (Smith et al., 1992).

Around the world, substance abuse has created additional victims. Unlike other drugs, crack cocaine quickly achieved a high rate of use and addiction among pregnant women and women of childbearing age. Its use has resulted in hundreds of thousands of drug-exposed babies, who are frequently born premature and suffering from damage to their nervous systems or have other complications (DuPont, 1991).

CASE STUDIES

The following two studies exemplify two different backgrounds where illegal drugs are used.

CASE STUDY 1
Weasel and the Logan 30

Weasel strolls down Logan Avenue amid scores of drug users, buyers, and sellers. He is pleased because his gang, the Logan 30, is making lots of money. Most of the drug users ignore Weasel, but the sellers are aware of his presence and are nervously deferential. Most of the drug sellers are addicts themselves, although some are just youngsters hoping to be as successful as Weasel. None of the sellers can afford to alienate Weasel.

Across the trash-strewn street, Mrs. Yoder looks out her apartment window with a mixture of disgust and fear. Although this street had always been poor, the neighborhood was clean and safe until a few years ago. Neighbors used to talk to each other and look out for one another. There was no graffiti and there were no shootings. The street lights worked, and the trash was picked up weekly. The Logan 30 was just a group of kids hanging out together back then. Like many of her longtime neighbors, Mrs. Yoder wonders how things got so out of hand. "Didn't the police and the city care about them?" She closes the blinds and watches the door.

Weasel is on a mission. He meets Shooter at the corner liquor store, which serves as the neighborhood's only source of food. There are no grocery stores anymore; bread and milk cost twice as much here as they do in the suburbs, and malt liquor is cheaper than soda. Weasel and Shooter pick up a package from the clerk, who tells them that it just arrived from Mexico and "hasn't been stepped on" yet. Shooter samples the package's contents while Weasel watches the door.

A police car slowly rolls up the street. For a moment, all but the most brazen drug dealers cease business. Officers Miller and Sanders watch. They know that as soon as they turn the corner, the drug market will return to life. Although they will make several arrests tonight, they know they will not make a dent in the illicit activities. They are frustrated and burned out. As they watch the users and sellers patiently wait, a call comes in on the radio. There's been a shooting at an apartment complex not far away. The police car speeds off with its lights flashing.

Hearing the nearby gunshots, Weasel and Shooter check their own guns. Their package is worth more than most people earn in a year, and they won't let their rivals take it without a fight. Guns are their only form of insurance, and violence unfortunately is a business necessity. Weasel and Shooter carefully walk down the street and distribute their product. When they finish, they will meet the rest of the Logan 30 in an abandoned house down the street. After they count the day's profits, the group will party into the next morning, getting high on drugs and alcohol (case study provided by the Midwest NASW Center on Violence, Development, and Substance Abuse).

CASE STUDY 2
Julie

Julie wakes up at 7:45 A.M. feeling slightly nauseated and with a headache from overdrinking and using cocaine at a party the night before. She will be late for work again (which makes twice this week) and is annoyed with herself for waking up late. She lights a cigarette and stumbles to the bathroom, reassuring herself that her boss will overlook her tardiness because she had a stellar performance review and has a solid attendance record. Julie views her occasional party nights as a means of compensating for her hard work and as a source of adventure in her otherwise mundane life.

At 26, Julie is the youngest corporate attorney at her company. She had no problem landing a high-paying job at the Fortune 500 company because she is a graduate of an Ivy League university and has great credentials. Julie enjoys the after-hour rituals that she and her colleagues have established to reward themselves for their accomplishments. After a hard day's work, they gather at the local bar for drinks (and sometimes cocaine on the side) and stimulating conversations before they head home. Julie enjoys feeling "buzzed" and care-free.

Julie began drinking beer and wine and smoking cigarettes in high school. In college she first experimented with marijuana and gradually moved on to other drugs, such as cocaine and ecstacy. As with her use of alcohol and cigarettes, Julie manages to confine her experimentation with drugs exclusively to social occasions. Besides hangovers, until now Julie has suffered no noticeable negative physical or social consequences from her use of substances. She believes that her use of illicit drugs is no different from her use of legal drugs.

Julie has always been a strong advocate for legalizing the sale and use of drugs. She thinks that the current U.S. drug laws are, at best, based on moralistic assumptions and that they are hypocritical, economics driven, and manipulated by political demagogues. When Julie debates this issue with friends, she points out that altering one's perception through the use of natural drugs is a behavior that has been part of virtually every culture since the earliest societies. Furthermore, the consequences of getting high are often determined by the social context, values, and norms of a society anyway. Julie concedes, however, that substance use is a problem for some people and could have dangerous consequences, such as accidents, crime, and violence. But, she argues, the War on Drugs is hypocritical in a society that legally consumes billions of dollars worth of alcohol and tobacco each year. Moreover, the U.S. government subsidizes these industries' efforts to sell their products overseas to the so-called Third World countries

(case study provided by the Midwest NASW Center on Violence, Development, and Substance Abuse).

ONE SOURCE OF HOPE: THE ENTREPRENEURIAL DEVELOPMENT INSTITUTE

The primary goal of the Entrepreneurial Development Institute (TEDI), based in Washington, DC, is to equip youths and their families in that city with the skills and resources necessary to become full stakeholders in the economic and social revitalization of their communities by establishing their own small businesses (TEDI, 1995). TEDI has a microloan fund available to students who have completed the first part of the training program and are ready to start their own businesses. Since 1991, 1,800 youths have been involved, and 85 business plans have been drawn up, creating over 650 jobs (personal communication with TEDI staff, August 1996). Of the adjudicated youths who make up 30 percent of the participants, TEDI boasts an amazing zero percent recidivism rate for drug-related offenses. Parents, teachers, and counselors claim that TEDI graduates get better grades, act more responsibly at home, and engage in long-term educational and career planning. TEDI proves that entrepreneurial education is a viable alternative to drugs and crime, a means of achieving economic self-sufficiency, and a pathway to academic excellence. TEDI is now planning to replicate its model in 18 other cities across the country.

CURTAILING DRUG–RELATED VIOLENCE THROUGH SUSTAINABLE HUMAN DEVELOPMENT

> Development alone will not be the solution to the narcotics problem, but it does provide a more adequate platform for dealing with the underlying causes. (Smith et al., 1992, p. 114)

The 1980s were characterized by the unrestrained consumption of resources by the rich countries of the global North, which intensified worldwide injustices and poverty. One result has been increasing alienation and loss of hope that fuel the use of drugs and violence (Korten, 1990). Sustainable human development, as an antidote to hopelessness, is the most effective means of getting at the root causes of the drug problem and reducing the production, trafficking, and consumption of illegal drugs.

Reducing Production

As Shuman and Harvey (1993) pointed out, a key reason why the aggressive law enforcement approach favored by the United States has not been effective is that it fails to recognize that growers have a different motive from international traffickers: survival. Poor farmers grow coca plants primarily because producing drug crops yields higher profits and guaranteed markets and hence provides an alternative to the abject poverty and governmental neglect that have plagued their communities for decades.

To curb production, farmers must have viable alternative ways of earning a decent living. Replacing coca with other agricultural produce will not be sufficient. Rather, ensuring the successful substitution of food crops for coca will depend on several factors, including local marketing systems that protect perishable crops; transportation to markets; steady buyers; the allowance of sufficient time for the new crops to take hold; and international policies that provide favorable trade, credit, infrastructure, and price conditions (*Narcotics and Development*, 1993).

According to the United Nations Development Pro-gramme (1994), it is unreasonable to expect the global South to bear most of the cost of clamping down on the production and export of illegal drugs because demand in the global North fuels the narcotics trade. Rather, the UN has recommended that countries in the global North should be generous in supporting sustainable human development programs for poor farmers, including assistance for farm equipment and small-scale loans.

Reducing Trafficking

International interdiction of narcotics trafficking has been minimally successful to date and requires a different approach. Currently, nations rely on primitive law enforcement networks to eradicate crops, to prevent large-scale laundering of drug profits, and to prosecute drug lords. In the absence of serious enforceable international drug laws, criminals simply move freely to countries with the weakest antidrug policies (Shuman & Harvey, 1993).

In the United States, youths will find it hard to resist the lure of the drug trade as long as they can make a hundred times more by selling drugs than by working at minimum-wage jobs that offer no health benefits and no chance of promotion. A social development approach is needed to combat the problem. Such an approach requires adequate educational opportunities, economic programs to bring businesses and industries back to poor communities, and improved community resources and infrastructure to support the healthy development of individuals and neighborhoods.

Reducing Consumption

Because drug addiction is a disease (and because drug-related crime is often associated with feeding addictions), the focus should be on preventing and treating substance abuse. A federally funded study by the RAND Corporation found that drug treatment is seven times more cost-effective in cutting the demand for cocaine than are local law enforcement efforts, 11 times more effective than border interdiction, and 22 times more effective than efforts to control foreign production ("Focus on Drug Treatment," 1994).

One drastic proposal put forth to reduce the consumption of illicit drugs is legalization. This is a risky proposition, however, because consumption may actually increase. Ultimately, the best solution seems to be to promote social and economic development in the global North and South as a means of strengthening families and communities, providing alternatives to drug use, and offering hope (UN Development Programme, 1994).

Funding Sustainable Human Development Strategies

Curtailing the drug epidemic requires long-term, multifaceted approaches that address its root causes. Implementing such approaches undoubtedly would be expensive. The irony is that the United States and the entire international community end up paying in any case—and they pay a lot more down the line than they would have paid up front (UN Development Programme, 1994). For $25 billion, which is half the cost American cities are now paying to curb crime, sickness, and other damages from the War on Drugs, the United States could pay every rural family in Latin America $1,000, the typical annual income for a coca farmer, not to grow coca (Shuman & Harvey, 1993).

Providing money for development in both the source countries of the global South and in underdeveloped areas in the consumer countries of the global North requires a change of priorities. The UN Development Programme (1994) proposed a 3 percent reduction in global military spending from 1995 to 2000, which would produce $85 billion in new funds for sustainable human development throughout the world. For development programs to succeed, however, they must meet the basic human needs of every person, expand economic opportunities for poor people, promote meaningful citizen participation, and protect the environment (*At the Crossroads*, 1995).

WHAT YOU CAN DO

- Learn more about the interdependent causes and consequences of the maldevelopment–substance abuse–violence cycle, using the information and references in part 5 as a start.

- Learn about solutions to the drug problem that focus on international cooperation to reduce both the supply and demand of illicit drugs.
- Develop a greater understanding of international development issues and use that understanding to advocate for programs that address the root causes of the drug problem: poverty and inequity.
- Advocate for the worldwide reduction in military expenditures to free up resources for development.

REFERENCES

Andelman, D. A. (1994). The drug money maze. *Foreign Affairs, 73,* 994–1008.

At the crossroads: The future of foreign aid (Occasional Paper No. 4). (1995). (Available from Bread for the World Institute, 1100 Wayne Avenue, Suite 1000, Silver Spring, MD 20910; phone 301-608-2400)

Atkinson, R. (1994, June 28). FBI chief urges Europeans to shift cold war resources to fight crime. *Washington Post,* p. A18.

Benjamin, P. (1990). A war on drugs can reduce violence in black neighborhoods. In J. Rohr (Ed.), *Violence in America: Opposing viewpoints* (pp. 80–85). San Diego: Greenhaven Press.

DuPont, R. (Ed.). (1991). *Crack cocaine: A challenge for prevention.* Washington, DC: U.S. Department of Health and Human Services.

Entrepreneurial Development Institute. (1995). *General organization overview.* (Available from the institute at 2025 I Street, NW, Suite 905, Washington, DC 20006; phone 202-822-8334)

Focus on drug treatment. (1994, June 16). *USA Today,* p. A12.

Golden, T. (1995, July 30). Mexican connection grows as cocaine supplier to U.S. *New York Times,* p. A1.

King, A., & Schneider, B. (1991). *The first global revolution.* New York: Pantheon Books.

Korten, D. (1990). *Getting to the 21st century: Voluntary actions and the global agenda.* West Hartford, CT: Kumarian Press.

Narcotics and development. (1993). Washington, DC: Panos Institute.

Office of National Drug Control Policy. (1995). *What America's users spend on illegal drugs, 1988–1993.* Washington, DC: Executive Office of the President.

Ostrowski, J. (1990). Repealing drug laws can reduce drug violence. In J. Rohr (Ed.), *Violence in America: Opposing viewpoints* (pp. 73–79). San Diego: Greenhaven Press.

Rohr, J. (1990). Preface to Chapter 2. In J. Rohr (Ed.), *Violence in America: Opposing viewpoints* (pp. 50–51). San Diego: Greenhaven Press.

Schemo, D. J. (1995, August 13). Colombia in crisis as drugs tar chief. *New York Times,* p. A12.

Schmoke, K. L. (1990). More law enforcement cannot reduce drug violence. In J. Rohr (Ed.), *Violence in America: Opposing viewpoints* (pp. 59–66). San Diego, CA: Greenhaven Press.

Shuman, M. H., & Harvey, H. (1993). *Security without war: A post–cold war foreign policy.* Boulder, CO: Westview Press.

Sims, C. (1995, July 11). Defying U.S. threat, Bolivians plant more coca. *New York Times,* p. A3.

Smith, M. L., Thongtham, C. N., Sadeque, N., Bravo, A. M., Rumrill, R., & Davila, A. (1992). *Why people grow drugs: Narcotics and development in the Third World.* Washington, DC: Panos Institute.

United Nations Development Programme. (1994). *Human development report, 1994.* New York: Oxford University Press.

U.S. Department of Justice. (1994). *Drugs and crime facts, 1994.* Washington, DC: U.S. Government Printing Office.

Van Soest, D., & Bryant, S. (1995). Violence reconceptualized for social work: The urban dilemma. *Social Work, 40,* 549–557.

Watson, R., Katel, P., Gutkin, S., Waller, D., Liu, M., & Spencer, R. (1993, December 13). Death on the spot: The end of a drug king. *Newsweek,* pp. 19–21.

ADDITIONAL RESOURCES

National Clearinghouse for Alcohol and
Drug Information
PO Box 2345
Rockville, MD 20852
Phone: 800-729-6686
A government agency that collects and provides information about narcotics in the United States.

Panos Institute
1025 T. Jefferson Street, NW, Suite 105
Washington, DC 20007
Phone: 202-965-5177
A research institute that publishes educational materials on issues of development, including the narcotics trade.

PART 6

SURVIVAL IS VICTORY

Rwandans fleeing the mass killing in their village are emotionally numb by the time they reach the border with Zaire. A Vietnam War veteran abuses alcohol and cannot hold down a job. A child becomes withdrawn and takes no interest in her schoolwork after her family is forced to move to a homeless shelter. Across national borders, people who have been traumatized share many of the same symptoms. All have experienced or witnessed overwhelming violence, whether it is structural violence (such as poverty, hunger, and homelessness), personal violence (such as mugging and rape), or institutional violence (such as war, genocide, state repression, and torture).

Part 6 explores three causes of trauma and the relationship between trauma and violence. It also examines strategies that have been used both in the United States and in the global South to heal victims of trauma.

WHAT IS TRAUMA?

Exposure to sudden, prolonged, or repeated experiences of a life-threatening nature may result in deep emotional wounding, or psychological trauma, for victims and witnesses. Such emotional injury often includes feelings of intense rage and powerlessness. The scenes and images of violence become permanently imprinted in the psyche, along with associated feelings of terror and anguish (Prigoff, 1995).

Posttraumatic stress disorder (PTSD) is a psychological condition that results from exposure to a traumatic experience that exceeds a person's ability to respond or cope effectively. Symptoms associated with PTSD include flashbacks (in which the victim repeatedly reexperiences the event in his or her mind), a numbing of responsiveness and an avoidance of situations associated with the trauma, and a tendency to overreact to loud noises or quick movements (American Psychiatric Association, 1994). Among those at risk for PTSD are political refugees; torture victims; combat veterans; and survivors of rape, incest, alcoholic families, assault, domestic violence, war, and natural disasters (Bedics, Rappe, & Rappe, 1991).

THREE CAUSES OF TRAUMA

War

Children who witness acts of violence during war often have images that haunt them for years. The international development agency Save the Children (*Children at War*, 1994) estimated that 10 million children who are living today around the world have experienced emotional stress caused by war. Like children who are exposed to conventional warfare, young people in the United States who live under conditions of chronic violence (for example, in neighborhoods where gang warfare and police crackdowns are common) may experience symptoms of trauma (Masser, 1992). Parents, too, can become traumatized. Studies have found that parents everywhere who are unable to provide a safe environment for their children sometimes lose confidence and become emotionally unresponsive (*Starting Points*, 1994).

In addition, war often affects entire communities and nations. The collective trauma caused by the dropping of the atomic bombs on Hiroshima and Nagasaki still haunts Japan. And in the former Yugoslavia, symptoms of trauma are pervasive in communities that have been ravaged by war.

Migration

Since the mid-1970s, more people than ever before have been forced to flee their homes as a result of political repression, war, torture, and other violent conditions. For example, the number of refugees worldwide jumped from 10.5 million in 1984 to 14.5 million in 1994 (United Nations High Commission for Refugees, 1993, 1995). Not only are the situations that provoked flight horrific, but the actual process of migration can be filled with terrors as well. Among refugee populations who have been uprooted from their homes, PTSD is common (Prigoff, 1995). Many refugees experience a profound sense of loss or defeat as a result of being separated from "all that is important and familiar: family, friends, language, culture" (Kahn, 1994, p. 21).

Homelessness

Conditions of poverty and deprivation are both physically and psychologically damaging. When people are unable to provide for their own basic needs and those of dependent family members, their sense of security is shattered. Homelessness, for example, deprives people of their right to security and is often traumatizing, especially for children (Prigoff, 1995). As Bassuk and Gallagher (1990) noted:

> Researchers have . . . reported that the majority of homeless children suffer from serious developmental, emotional, and learning problems. . . . For preschoolers, these five years span critical developmental stages. Extended trauma during this time may initiate a cycle of underachievement and emotional problems that cannot readily be reversed. (p. 32)

A survey conducted in 30 U.S. cities found that families with children account for 39 percent of the homeless population and that children account for just over one-quarter of the homeless population (Waxman, 1994).

THE EFFECTS OF UNRESOLVED TRAUMA: ROADBLOCKS TO DEVELOPMENT

If left untreated, trauma may prevent individuals from moving forward and living their lives to their full potential. Long-term effects of unresolved trauma include PTSD, low self-esteem, depression, chemical dependence, and violent behavior (California NASW chapter Center, 1994). Some common responses of traumatized individuals are flight response, identification with the oppressor, and truncated moral development.

Flight Response

Sometimes trauma evokes responses that initially function as a form of self-protection. The flight response, for example, involves the avoidance of painful memories; the trauma is hidden and denied as a defense against shame or self-blame (Figley, 1995; Herman, 1992). Denial prevents individuals from getting the help they need to address and cope with their current realities. In the absence of emotional healing, the protective response is likely to become rigid and chronic, resulting in self-defeating patterns of behavior (California NASW chapter Center, 1994).

Identification with the Aggressor

Traumatized individuals often suffer devastating assaults to self-esteem and increased helplessness and dependence as a result of their inability to protect themselves. Unless their trust is restored through psychological healing, they may adopt the dominators' perspective of themselves, forming a "traumatic bond" with their oppressors and internalizing or redirecting their aggression toward others who are similar to them (Dutton & Painter, 1993).

Role reversal, in which a former powerless victim assumes the attributes of the aggressor, is a critical dynamic in the cycle of violence. The former victim may provoke repeated abuse or reverse the roles, so the victim becomes the victimizer. Such learned and repeated patterns of behavior have been documented in cases of family violence, as well as physical assaults with deadly weapons (California NASW chapter Center, 1994). Violent acts—which may first seem to be irrational when considered as isolated incidents—are often understandable as the symptoms of painful, humiliating, and shameful experiences of violence from which the victims have not recovered (Kordon & Edelman, 1986).

Truncated Moral Development

Chronic violence has been linked to truncated moral development in several cases. Fields's (1987) research in Northern Ireland and the Middle East, for example, revealed that children who live in violent communities remain at more primitive stages of moral development than do other children. If adults, such as parents and teachers, do not model higher moral reasoning, then it is likely that moral development will not occur.

TOWARD SOLUTION: APPROACHES TO HEALING

Empowerment

Empowerment approaches to treating trauma, including self-help groups and community-based services, allow individuals, families, and communities to make peace with the past and to regain control of their lives. Victims can be empowered by developing trust, speaking the truth, and expressing grief.

Developing trust. Confidentiality and a safe, caring environment are essential to help trauma victims search for forgotten and unhappy memories and to rediscover a sense of their own power. Traumatized people often find it easier to share their feelings in a self-help group in which other members have had similar experiences (Prigoff, 1993).

Speaking the truth. The full disclosure of available facts about a traumatizing event and associated feelings is crucial for recovery. If disclosed, feelings of anxiety, powerlessness, pain, and fear are likely to be defused and diminished over time and to become part of a conscious life history and the development of identity (Prigoff, 1993).

Expressing grief. Grieving and accepting losses—of other people, of trust, of safety, and of the meaning of life—are critical components of psychic healing (California NASW chapter Center, 1994). In the global South, communities use unique interventions to encourage people to come to terms with their grief. These interventions may be based on cultural rituals and traditions, ceremonies, spiritual experiences, drama, dance, storytelling, artwork, music, and other group activities (Prigoff, 1995).

Community Cooperation

Because the healing process requires social supports and connectedness to others, it can be powerful when communities draw on their own resources to heal from violence and trauma (Poole, 1993; Prigoff, 1995). Here are two examples:

El Salvador. In a closed refugee camp in El Salvador, members divided responsibilities for child care, agriculture, food preparation, sewing, and carpentry so that everyone contributed to the survival and well-being of the community. New arrivals were assigned integral roles in the settlement to make them feel at home. Salvadoran psychologists who worked with this camp reported significant positive psychosocial results (Roe, 1992).

United States. Residents of five underdeveloped neighborhoods in Kansas City are working to rebuild their communities by offering support to one another. "Block leaders" receive limited financial compensation to spend time with young people and their parents, offering such services as help with homework, field trips, wake-up calls, home visits, and advocacy at school. They are demonstrating that neighbors can reduce crime and repair the fabric of their own communities, block by block (Pittman, 1995).

Apology and Forgiveness

Apologies by people or nations that have caused trauma to others are an important and powerful step on the path to healing (Kahn, 1994). When former South African president F. W. de Klerk offered a deep and dramatic apology for apartheid in April 1993, he helped pave the way for a future for South Africa. Similarly, former Governor of Alabama George Wallace accomplished what the United States as a nation has not yet achieved. Once an avowed segregationist who ordered dogs and fire hoses to be turned on African American civil rights demonstrators, he eventually came to the realization that he was wrong and publicly apologized for his former position. In 1982, he ran for a fourth term. In a dramatic testament to generosity and forgiveness, it was the African American vote that carried him (Lehigh, 1995).

Researchers view interpersonal forgiveness as the smallest unit of peacemaking. Moreover, forgiveness is coming to be seen as a legitimate method of international conflict resolution (personal correspondence with Beverly Flanigan, coordinator, National Conference on Forgiveness, School of Social Work, University of Wisconsin-Madison, April 27, 1995). Whether between individuals, groups, or nations, apologies for former wrongs (in tandem with a conciliatory forgiver) tend to soften the memory of former conflict and to promote an atmosphere from which mending and progress can occur (Kahn, 1994).

Conscientiousness and Democracy Building

For oppressed peoples, an important part of the healing process is their ability to analyze the political and social forces that contributed to their trauma in the first place and then to take action to end inequality. This kind of self-awareness and participation is essential for a true and flourishing democracy, liberty, and self-determination (Prigoff, 1993).

Real change and healing may mandate a shift in the traditional power structures of the past, enabling victims to gain more control over their lives and ensuring that atrocities are not repeated. Combatting helplessness at all levels and replacing it with hope and action for a better future are key elements in the complete recovery from trauma.

One inspiring story of the power of individuals to effect change comes from Guatemala. Motivated by the "disappearance" of their loved ones by government security forces, surviving relatives united to form El GAM—the Mutual Support Group for Relatives of the Disappeared. The founders had met by chance while looking for their sons and husbands in prisons and morgues. They exchanged names, phone numbers, and support. At the first official meeting in 1985, 25 women came together. One member recalled, "We all got up and told our personal stories. It was very emotional" (Guatemala, 1985, p. 10).

Subsequently, they petitioned and demonstrated in the streets, demanding to know what had happened to their family members. As the disappearances continued, the membership in El GAM swelled to nearly 1,000. For their courageous and selfless efforts to gain justice in the face of adversity, they have received international recognition and support. Today, they continue to work for democracy, justice, and human rights. Their leader and one of the original founders, Nineth Montenegro de García, was recently elected to the Guatemalan Parliament under a new, progressive political party comprised of a wide range of organizations that work for social justice and human rights (PBI/USA Report, 1996).

CASE STUDIES

The first case study illustrates the impact of trauma on one person. The other four case studies illustrate the different ways that people throughout the world are healing from violence-related trauma.

CASE STUDY 1
Initial Interview with H

H grew up in a small town in Cambodia where he led a happy and secure life with his parents, four sisters, and two brothers. When Pol Pot came to power, one of his sisters and his father were killed. His mother died of sickness a few months later. H was forced to separate from his siblings, whom he never heard from again. He was forced to labor long hours without food. He became emaciated, although he did not suffer any specific injuries. H remembered seeing people killed routinely and corpses being "piled up." In 1977, H escaped to Thailand, where he was a refugee for two years before he came to the United States at age 15.

After a three-year period of adjustment in the United States, H was referred to a school social worker because his grades were dropping owing to his inability to concentrate and sit still in class and because he was absent a great deal from school. When he was interviewed by the social worker, he became angry and irritable when asked about his feelings. Then he reluctantly said that he felt sad most of the time. When asked what his life had been like since he left Cambodia, H seemed close to tears. He said he had no trouble thinking about Cambodia, but he had never discussed what had happened there. He seemed angry and looked away when he described some early events.

H said that when people were killed, they were dumped in a mass grave and that he witnessed these killings every day for a while. He also said that he sometimes remembered traumatic events when he did not want to; for example, the Fourth of July fireworks brought back the memory of his father being shot. Throughout the interview, H seemed agitated and tapped his foot on the floor. (Adapted from Van Soest, 1992, p. 83)

CASE STUDY 2
The Circle of Healing

Aboriginal people in Manitoba, Canada, are using the Circle of Healing to address the problem of violence in their communities (MATCH International Centre, 1994). The circle was started by five or six women from the Hollow Water Reserve who began meeting secretly to share their problems and later opened their discussions to the community. The group connected the psychological, emotional, and physical violence they were subjected to with the economic, social, and political underdevelopment of their community. They realized that unless violence was dealt with, their community could not move forward. In 1987, the group decided to tackle sexual abuse directly when two rapists returned to the reserve after spending three years in jail and raped again. The people of the reserve turned to the Circle of Healing, a method as old as native society.

The Circle of Healing involves treating the entire community to exorcise the pervasive illness of violence through the use of two treatment programs:

a five-day intensive therapy program and a 13-step process that takes two to five years. The circle insists that an offender must admit his or her responsibility before it gets involved, on the principle that until the victimizer is healed, there will be more victims.

A key to the circle's power of healing is a special gathering at which members of the community, the victim, the abuser, and family members come together to face the crime. First, the abuser has to acknowledge the crime publicly. Then members of the community tell the abuser how they feel about what happened and offer their support for healing. They also speak to the victim and the families involved.

The abuser is given a "healing contract" that sets out his or her punishment—usually community work—and arrangements are made to protect the victim. When the contract expires, a cleansing ceremony is held to symbolize the return of balance to the abuser, the family, and the community. At this point, healing is considered to be complete, and the crime is to be forgotten.

CASE STUDY 3
Ms. G

Ms. G is a 72-year-old widow who has congestive heart failure. She lives with her 50-year-old son, Mr. G, and his family, which consists of his second wife, age 35, and their three young children ages two, three, and five. Ms. G was born in a small, rural community in a Central American country but raised her seven children in an urban area. Her husband worked as a laborer, and it was a continuous struggle to provide the basic necessities for the family, which also included her husband's widowed mother. Ms. G stated that her religious faith and belief that her sons would one day be successful sustained her through the hard times. Since her husband died in 1985, she has lived with her second son.

For more than a decade, Ms. G's native country has been experiencing political upheaval; the regime in power has been fighting rebel forces. Ms. G's two younger sons and one of her grandchildren were killed in the fighting. Mr. G emigrated with his family to the United States in 1991, and Ms. G joined them later that year. She has had difficulty adjusting and complains to her son and daughter-in-law, whom she thinks should take better care of her. Ms. G lacks medical insurance, and her son has refused to arrange and pay for the oxygen tank that she needs.

When Ms. G recently fell in a store, gasping for breath, she was taken to a nearby hospital and treated. A social worker was called in to speak with Ms. G and her son. A nurse's aide interpreted for Ms. G and her son, and it was determined that Mr. G was afraid to pay for his mother's care because his wife would be angry that their children would then have to do without. Ms. G stated that although she believed her son should care for her, she had seen her husband, children, and grandchild all die and that it was her turn to die. The social worker contacted a local priest who spoke the native language of Mr. and Ms. G. He was able to convince the Gs that Ms. G's respiratory problems could be averted and asked Ms. G to come talk with him at the church about her sadness over her relatives' deaths. (Case study contributed by Linda Vinton, associate professor, School of Social Work, Florida State University, Tallahassee; used with permission)

CASE STUDY 4
A Program for Traumatized Mozambican Women and Children

A multifaceted program was developed in Zambia in an attempt to meet the psychosocial needs of Mozambican women and children who had experienced many horrors before fleeing their country. Women's clubs were organized to provide mutual aid and understanding among women who had experienced similar traumas and to strengthen the women's parenting and homemaking skills. A program was developed around groups of four or five women who were known to be people from whom others sought assistance. These women were given support and training to develop cocounseling models. A similar program was requested and established for men (Ressler, Tortorici, & Marcelino, 1993).

A pilot program was initiated to involve village children who had been traumatized in structured play. In addition, a clinic-based infant-stimulation program was organized to encourage mothers to play with and stimulate their children after it was observed that the mothers, especially those who had experienced trauma, were unresponsive to their children and that some children were withdrawn.

A school-based program was developed to train preschool and elementary school teachers to be more aware of the special needs of traumatized children and to promote a more caring and supportive classroom environment for the children. Age-appropriate activities for the children included songs, storytelling, role-plays, and group discussions and activities through which children could recall their experiences and feelings in a safe and supportive environment.

Another aspect of the program that the organizers considered to be important was the "sensitization" of agency workers, village leaders, and others to the special needs of traumatized individuals and the provision of assistance in resolving these individuals' difficulties (Ressler et al., 1993).

CASE STUDY 5
Learning to Cry in the Same Room

Nancy Baron, a clinical psychologist based in Boston, spent two years exploring ways in which psychology can be used to help war widows and children who have been displaced by civil strife in Sri Lanka. She began by helping a small non-governmental organization that was working with war widows, most of whom were under age 30 and some of whom had up to eight children. Many of the displaced families had been in camps for up to four years. . . .

[Baron] realized that in Sri Lanka she was working with a society that does not give people an opportunity to express sadness . . . "The society tries to make people forget. We gave them an opportunity to explore their feelings." She started with a group of perhaps 30 war widows from the four ethnic factions affected by the fighting. She used art to overcome language barriers. "They drew an early childhood that was happy, a young adulthood that was happy and then the beginning of the trouble after the death of the husband. . . . The women were able to sit together and say that each group was responsible for killing each other's husbands. Everyone was crying, and they were able to hug each other."

One woman did not cry. She pointed to the scar on her face and said that her husband had stabbed her. She was relieved when he was killed. "The women empathized with her. They could talk about the experience" (Mann, 1994).

REFERENCES

American Psychiatric Association. (1994). *Diagnostic and statistical manual of mental disorders* (4th ed.). Washington, DC: Author.

Bassuk, E. L., & Gallagher, E. M. (1990). The impact of homelessness on children. In N. A. Boxill (Ed.), *Homeless children: The watchers and the waiters* (pp. 19–34). New York: Haworth Press.

Bedics, B. C., Rappe, P. T., & Rappe, L. O. (1991). Preparing BSW professionals for identifying and salvaging victims of post traumatic stress disorder. In B. Shank (Ed.), *B.S.W. education for practice: Reality and fantasy. Refereed papers from the ninth annual BPD Conference, Orlando, Florida* (pp. 94–100). St. Paul, MN: University of St. Thomas.

California NASW chapter Center on Trauma, Violence, and Development. (1994). [Report submitted to the Violence and Development Project]. Sacramento: Author.

Children at war. (1994). (Available from Save the Children, 52 Wilton Road, Westport, CT 06880; phone 203-221-4000)

Dutton, D. G., & Painter, S. (1993). Emotional attachments in abusive relationships: A test of traumatic bonding theory. *Violence and Victims, 8,* 105–120.

Fields, R. (1987, October 25). *Terrorized into terrorist: Sequelae of PTSD in young victims.* Paper presented at the meeting of the Society for Traumatic Stress Studies, New York City.

Figley, C. R. (1995). *Compassion fatigue: Secondary traumatic stress disorder—Theory, research and treatment.* New York: Brunner/Mazel.

Guatemala: The group for mutual support. (1985). New York: Americas Watch.

Herman, J. L. (1992). *Trauma and recovery.* New York: Basic Books.

Kahn, A. B. (1994, August 22). *Violence and social development between conflicting groups.* Unpublished manuscript, California NASW Center on Trauma, Violence, and Development, Sacramento.

Kordon, D. R., & Edelman, L. L. (1986). *Efectos psicologicos de la represion politica.* Buenos Aires: Sudamericana/Planeta.

Lehigh, S. (1995, July 16). The art of saying "I'm sorry." *Boston Globe,* pp. 65, 67.

Mann, J. (1994, August 10). Learning to cry in the same room. *Washington Post,* p. E15.

Masser, D. (1992). Psychological functioning of Central American refugee children. *Child Welfare, 71,* 439–456.

MATCH International Centre. (1994). The Circle of Healing: Aboriginal women organizing in Canada. In M. Davies (Ed.), *Women and violence: Realities and responses worldwide* (pp. 234–239). Atlantic Highlands, NJ: Zed Books.

PBI/USA Report. (1996, March). [Newsletter]. (Available from Peace Brigades International/ USA, 2642 College Avenue, Berkeley, CA 94704; phone 510-540-0749)

Pittman, K. (1995, May–June). Rebuilding community, block by block. *Youth Today,* p. 46.

Poole, W. (1993). *The heart of healing: Institute of Noetic Sciences.* Atlanta: Turner.

Prigoff, A. (1993). *Violence, trauma, loss and deprivation: Psychological wounds and processes of healing.* Paper presented at the 10th Annual North America-Nicaragua Health Colloquium, Managua.

Prigoff, A. (1995). *Healing and recovery from psychological trauma, with individuals, families and communities.* Unpublished manuscript, School of

Social Work, California State University, Sacramento.

Ressler, E. M., Tortorici, J., & Marcelino, A. (1993). *Children in war: A guide to the provision of services*. New York: UNICEF.

Roe, M. (1992). Displaced women in settings of continuing armed conflict. *Women and Therapy*, *13*(1–2), 89–102.

Starting points: Meeting the needs of your youngest children (Report of the Carnegie Task Force on Meeting the Needs of Young Children). (1994, April). New York: Carnegie Corporation.

United Nations High Commission for Refugees. (1993). *The challenge of protection*. New York: United Nations.

United Nations High Commission for Refugees. (1995). *Populations of concern to UNHCR*. New York: United Nations.

Van Soest, D. (1992). *Incorporating peace and social justice into the social work curriculum*. Washington, DC: Office of Peace and International Affairs, National Association of Social Workers.

Waxman, L. (1994). *A status report on hunger and homelessness in America's cities*. Washington, DC: U.S. Conference of Mayors.

ADDITIONAL RESOURCES

Amnesty International, USA
322 Eighth Avenue
New York, NY 10001
Phone: 212-807-8400
   An organization that works for the release of all prisoners of conscience and an end to torture and executions.

Save the Children
52 Wilton Road
Westport, CT 06880
Phone: 203-221-4000
   An organization that works with child victims of war in more than 25 countries. It trains social workers to provide treatment for emotional distress and to conduct programs for families.

UNICEF, global South malnutrition report, 16

United Nations (UN)
    Declaration for Social Development, 18
    Department of Public Information, 6
    Development Programme (poverty recommendations), 12–13
    International Decade of the World's Indigenous People, 36
    Universal Declaration of Human Rights, 18
    World Summit for Social Development (Copenhagen), 18

United States
    battery to women in, 22
    cocaine use in, 39, 41
    development efforts needed in, 3
    foreign assistance (advantages and myths of), 17
    foreign assistance budget, 2, 10
    health insurance availability in, 10
    history of ethnoviolence in, 33–34
    hunger in, 15
    infant mortality in, 3
    literacy survey, 3
    military expenditures, 4
    poverty in, 9, 11
    trade with poor countries (myths about), 17
    welfare budget (1995), 10

United States Committee for Refugees, 37

United Way, racial injustice and, 36

Universal Declaration of Human Rights (UN), 18

Urbanization, as precipitant of violence, 24

V

Violence (overview). *See also* Children, violence against; Drug abuse; Ethnoviolence; Poverty; Trauma; Women, violence against
    defined, 2–3
    effects of on development, 4
    effects of worldwide, 1
    threats to personal security and social stability, 2–3

Violence and Development Project, expanding definition of violence, 2

W

Wallace, George, 50

Wangari, Maathai, case study of, 13

War. *See* Militarism

Weasel and the Logan 30, drug abuse case study of, 42

White supremacist movement, 33

Women, violence against
    Annapurna Mahila Mandal case study, 27–28
    changing political and economic systems (effects of), 24
    development that addresses, 25–26
    domestic violence, 23–24
    gender-sensitive development, 25
    global problem of (statistics), 21–22
    linking family structure with violence and violence prevention case study, 26–27
    male domination, 23
    militarism and, 23
    1975 International Women's Year World Conference (Mexico City), 21
    1980 Mid-Decade World Conference for Women (Copenhagen), 21
    1985 World Conference on Women (Nairobi), 21
    raising the status of women, 24
    sustainable human development as antidote to, 24–25
    underdevelopment as precipitant of, 24
    women healing from violence in Nicaragua case study, 26

Women's Commission for Refugee Women and Children, 30

Working Women's Forum (Madras, India), 23

World. *See also* Global South; United Nations; United States
    development inequities in, 3–4
    global wealth disparity, 4–5, 9
    population/income breakdown, 2
    poverty rates, 9

World Conference on Women (Nairobi, 1985), 21

World Development Report, 7

World Military and Social Expenditures, 7

World Summit on Children, 5

World Summit for Social Development, 5

World-Watch Institute, violence against women, 21

Y

Yunus, Muhammad, 4, 14

Jane Crosby is director of the Violence and Development Project for the National Association of Social Workers. She received her master's of social work degree from Boston University in 1991. She previously worked at Oxfam America, an international development agency, where she directed the national education and fundraising hunger campaign, Fast for a World Harvest.

Dorothy Van Soest, DSW, is associate dean and associate professor at the School of Social Work, University of Texas at Austin. She has authored several articles and chapters on issues related to violence, peace, social justice, and development, as well as the book *Incorporating Peace and Social Justice into the Social Work Curriculum* (NASW, 1992). Her forthcoming book, *The Global Crisis of Violence: Common Problems, Universal Consequences, Shared Solutions*, will be published by the NASW Press in 1997. She is former director of the NASW Violence and Development Project.

Cover and interior designed by Watermark Design.
Composed by Long-Run Publications
in Goudy and Univers.
Printed by Graphic Communications, Inc. on 60# Windsor Offset.